Laughter and Praise for

THE WOMAN WHO IS ALWAYS TAN AND HAS A FLAT STOMACH

"A hilarious take on all those annoying icons of mother-hood...It's refreshing to read a book that articulates what all of us really feel: Perfect people are annoying."

—MomCentral.com

"Not only will women love this book—I loved it too! Hilarious!" —Scott Patrick, former cohost of the Denver TV show *Colorado & Co.*

"A humorous look at everyday problems and people—you know, those annoying ones, those perfect ones."

—ArmchairInterviews.com

"Lauren Allison and Lisa Perry have written a book that all of us 'normal' women will love. Just reading through the chapter titles had me laughing out loud."

—Jane London, cohost of Denver radio Mix 100, *Dom and Jane and the Big Mix Morning Show*

"This is truly one of the funniest books I have ever read!"

—Amy Oliver, *The Amy Oliver Show*, KFKA Radio

THE
WOMAN WHO IS
ALWAYS TAN
AND HAS A
FLAT STOMACH

AND OTHER
ANNOYING PEOPLE

Lauren Allison and **Lisa Perry**

GRAND CENTRAL
PUBLISHING

NEW YORK   BOSTON

Grand Central Publishing
Hachette Book Group USA
237 Park Avenue
New York, NY 10017

Visit our Web site at www.HachetteBookGroupUSA.com.

Printed in the United States of America

First Grand Central Publishing Edition: March 2008
Originally published by Castle Pines Publishing, Castle Rock, CO
10 9 8 7 6 5 4 3 2 1

Grand Central Publishing is a division of Hachette Book Group USA, Inc.
The Grand Central Publishing name and logo is a trademark of Hachette Book Group, Inc.

Library of Congress Cataloging-in-Publication Data

Allison, Lauren.
    The woman who is always tan and has a flat stomach : and other annoying people / Lauren Allison and Lisa Perry.—1st ed.
        p. cm.
    ISBN-13: 978-0-446-69963-1
    ISBN-10: 0-446-69963-2
    1. Characters and characteristics—Humor.   2. Perfectionism (Personality trait)—Humor.   I. Perry, Lisa   II. Title.
PN6231.C27A45 2008
818'.602—dc22

                                                            2007014148

Book design and text composition by Stratford Publishing Services, a TexTech Company

Acknowledgments

We would like to thank our editor, Emily Griffin, for her dedication, professionalism, and enthusiasm for our book. We are very fortunate to have an agent, David Forrer, who has a ready mix of good judgment and great sense of humor; he and the staff at Inkwell Management have been invaluable to us throughout the process of publishing *The Woman Who Is Always Tan*. We would also like to thank our "perfect" friends out there who let us write about them; you know who you are. Without you, our self-esteem would never have plummeted and we never would have written about our many inadequacies. And we would like to thank our families, who have been supportive throughout it all.

THE
WOMAN WHO IS
ALWAYS TAN
AND HAS A
FLAT STOMACH

1

The Perfect Brownie Leader Who Uses Global Positioning Satellites on the Camping Trip to E-mail Photos to the Parents

I always find perfect people to be annoying, but the Perfect Brownie Leader is probably at the top of my list. The first year my daughter Caroline was in Brownies I was happy to be the troop leader. Granted, we did nothing too creative, nor did we do anything suggested in the manual. Mainly, we hung out at Dairy Queen.

But the next year, I was asked to merge my troop with another troop. I invited the other Brownie leader over for tea and she got right down to business. "What's been your troop motto, Lauren?" The Perfect Brownie Leader had an entire checklist to go through.

I said with pride, "Our troop motto is 'You can marry more money in one minute than you can make in a lifetime.'"

The Perfect Brownie Leader looked horrified. She said, "Well, *our* motto is 'Ask not what your country can do for you; ask what you can do for your country.'"

I slumped down in my chair. I thought I'd change the subject so I asked, "What day of the week shall we meet?"

She said, "Mondays won't work, because I'm involved with the United Nations Middle East peace talks every Monday."

I couldn't believe how much fun I was having.

She continued, "What uniforms have you been wearing? We should all try to be the same."

"Gosh!" I stammered. "My girls felt that an enforced uniform rule might stifle our creativity." I didn't mention that I had lost the order form.

"No problem. I'll convince your girls to wear the regulation uniforms. Okay, next." She was busy writing notes. "What have you planned for your first indoor project this year?"

I brightened at this. "We *do* have that much worked out. We want to make Christmas wreaths out of egg cartons."

"But Christmas is four months away." The Perfect Brownie Leader had some point to make. "It's only the end of August."

"It typically takes us about that long to finish a project," I replied weakly.

"Our Christmas project is to go to my home ceramics studio, throw platters on the potter's wheel, decorate and fire them. That can all be done in December."

"Wow, that sounds great. We can do the egg cartons another season."

Ignoring my comment, she glanced at her list again. "What cultural events do you have planned?"

"That's easy," I said. "Last year we went to Skate Town Roller Rink. They have the greatest cotton candy there—the blue stuff—and a little write-up on the concrete wall by the concession stand about how cotton candy was invented. It's very interesting."

She looked as if she was trying to comprehend what I'd just said. Finally, she said, "I see." She cleared her throat.

"I've arranged for a private tour and reception at the City Art Museum."

"A private tour! How did you manage that?"

"Oh," the Perfect Brownie Leader remarked, making an attempt at modesty. "I have a couple of my latest paintings there on loan. I'm into postmodern non-subjective oils, using a palette-knife technique."

"Fine," I said with a sigh. I decided to just throw in the towel.

———————

The weekend of our first big camping trip arrived. For the first time, I got to meet the Perfect Brownie Leader's husband, who was wearing camouflage fatigues. She said, "He's an ex–Navy SEAL, so he was even able to teach me a few things. For our honeymoon, we went on an Outward Bound survival experience in the Canadian tundra."

I went numb. They had gone on an Outward Bound survival experience in the Canadian tundra for their honeymoon? Oh, great, I thought, I'm going to have to find a way out of here. Perhaps I could say I was coming down with West Nile virus; surely I could use one of the mosquito bites I had gotten in the past hour to my advantage.

My thoughts were interrupted by the Perfect Brownie Leader saying, "Everyone line up for a group picture."

Just that morning I'd found the cheap disposable camera I'd lost last spring. "Let's finish this roll," I said to the girls. "I think our last Skate Town outing is on here."

The Perfect Brownie Leader pulled out her digital camera. After taking a dozen shots, she hooked up her laptop computer to her all-terrain Jeep battery. Then, using GPS technology, she sent the pictures to the girls' parents. Finally, she took my film, rolled down shades in the back of her Jeep, and processed my pictures.

Even the blue from the cotton candy at Skate Town came out brilliantly.

I must admit, the day passed pleasantly enough. We had nature hikes and sing-alongs. By mid-afternoon the girls were referring to poison ivy and poison oak by their Latin names. During the songfest, the Perfect Brownie Leader played the electric keyboard she had hooked up to the Jeep battery while her husband played the banjo and harmonica simultaneously.

A wonderful dinner cooked by the Perfect Brownie Leader's husband followed. He served filet mignon, roasted potatoes with sour cream and chives, and a chocolate soufflé done right over the campfire. Then an incredible piece of luck happened. One of the little campers felt sick and wanted to go home. Desperately I tried to get up on my feet so I could volunteer to take her home (this took several tries because of the way the dinner weighed me down).

The Perfect Brownie Leader was concern itself. Did I really not mind giving up the rest of the weekend? It seemed to be taken for granted I wasn't returning. How lucky I hadn't bothered to unpack.

2

The Nutrition Mom Who Needs to Be Resuscitated After Finding Out You Fed Her Child a Hot Dog

Nutrition Moms can be annoying; however, if the truth be told, I am quite sure that *I* am more annoying to *them* than vice versa. One day a mom asked if I'd like to have lunch with her. Little did I know that she was actually a Nutrition Mom. After we were seated at the restaurant, I ordered a diet soda and watched her pupils dilate to the size of nine-grain bagels.

I asked, "What's wrong?"

"You're not going to actually drink that, are you?"

"Sure, why not?"

"Oh, it's just a little thing called *saccharin,* which causes mice to roll over on their backs with their little feet in the air as they gasp their last breath."

She then ordered a boneless, skinless chicken breast, asparagus, and a salad with no dressing.

I ordered a double bacon-wrapped bratwurst with extra cheese on a white bun with supersize fries. The waiter asked, "Would you like a salad?"

"What's in it?"

"Organic collard greens, red chard, arugula, and red leaf lettuce with a low-fat dressing made with heart-healthy canola oil."

"Nah. I'll just have some iceberg lettuce with extra Thousand Island dressing."

The Nutrition Mom gagged, and the waiter left smiling.

The Nutrition Mom asked me what I'd been doing lately.

I thought a minute. "Well, on Friday night we went to a restaurant whose specialty is charred ham fat and it was delicious. Then on Saturday night we stayed home and my husband grilled one-pound steaks for each of us, with seven-cheese au gratin potatoes, corn pudding, rice pudding, and chocolate pudding for dessert. Afterward, we ate Cool Whip right out of the carton. It comes in chocolate flavor now. What have you been doing?"

She looked as if she was trying to process what I'd just said. Finally she rallied. "I went to the opening of the new Health Foods last week. It's so refreshing to shop somewhere where you know that everything is organic."

My mind drifted off to the three-pound package of butterscotch cookies I'd just bought at Sam's Club. They were still in the car, unfortunately.

When our waiter arrived with our salads, I leaned over and looked at her. "Which is the arugula? I don't think I've ever had that."

The Nutrition Mom pointed it out with her fork.

I said, "Just this morning I noticed the same stuff growing by my front sidewalk. I hit it with Roundup."

I asked if she had tried any new recipes lately. She said

that her sister had just given her a great tofu steak recipe with a vegetarian barbecue sauce.

I brightened. "I just tried something new, too. I used pork fat to make beef fondue. It was fabulous. You'd be surprised how much flavor pork fat adds to chuck beef if you don't cook it too long."

She closed her eyes tightly and didn't open them again for quite a few seconds.

Our food arrived. To her dismay, the chicken breast had been cooked with the skin on. "Oh, dear," she sighed, "they always forget to remove the skin."

"No problem, I'll eat it. That's the only part of the chicken I ever eat anyway." She passed it over.

She said, "By the way, next week I'll be out of town at the Mother's March on Washington for the Elimination of Partially Hydrogenated Vegetable Oils."

"Cool." I was impressed. "What's partially hydrogenated vegetable oil?"

"It happens to be one of the worst things you can eat. It's in all kinds of crackers, cookies, cakes, frostings, candy, even pancake mix."

"Good for you. How great to stand up for something you really believe in."

"Yes," she said. "It'd be wonderful to get companies to eliminate hydrogenated vegetable oils. Actually, in terms of fat, butter is better for you."

Surprised, I exclaimed, "Butter is better for you?" Now she was talking about something I could really endorse.

"Much better," she assured me.

"Great. I eat it straight sometimes. I just love butter."

"Then you should go with me to Washington. We need one more person to hold up a sign."

"What would my sign say?" I asked. "Would it have anything to do with butter?"

"As a matter of fact, it would. We need someone to hold the sign that says, GET OFF YOUR LARD ASS AND EAT BUTTER. Would you be interested?"

I smiled. "That sign has my name written all over it."

3

The Husband Who Takes It Personally When Someone Steals His Luggage and Then Returns It Without Taking Anything

My husband Michael and I recently stayed at a hotel in Miami but, to our dismay, while checking in, we found that one of our bags was missing. After examining our remaining bags, we realized that it was the one containing Michael's clothes.

We told the concierge, Armand, who immediately notified hotel security.

We went up to our room. As we began to unpack our bags, Armand knocked at our door and said that security had found our missing bag. He wanted Michael to check to make sure everything was there.

I said, "Check to see if that new cashmere sweater I just bought you is in there."

"It's here."

"How about all your shirts?"

"Yes," he replied, a little tersely.

"What about that new jacket?"

He stated indignantly, "They didn't take anything."

"Michael, why do you sound so upset?"

"I'm beginning to get the picture here."

Armand and I both looked at him, wondering what he meant.

"It means that my clothes just aren't good enough for the crook who took my bag."

We looked at him in disbelief.

He went on, "It means that my clothes weren't up to his standards."

"Mr. Perry, it doesn't have to mean that at all," Armand said, trying to placate him. "Maybe your clothes weren't his size."

"A large sweater would fit most people. So don't tell me that."

I said, "You don't have to take this so personally."

"How would you feel if your clothes weren't good enough for some thief? I don't see how you wouldn't take it personally."

I said, *"No one stole anything from you. This is good."*

"Well, my things are just as good as anyone else's. My clothes have been cast aside as inferior by some fashion-conscious crook."

Armand said, "Excuse me, but it's possible that you're right. Now let me ask you this, Mr. Perry: have you ever had your color wheel done? You know, where you have a professional skin and makeup artist determine what colors you should wear according to your skin tones? Maybe the colors on your color wheel and the colors on the color wheel of the thief are different from one another."

Michael pulled me aside and said in a hushed voice, "What is he talking about?"

I whispered back. "He just said that maybe the thief didn't like the color of your clothes."

Armand said, "You know, according to your skin tones, you should be wearing warm colors—like peaches and golds and rich browns. What are the colors of your clothes?"

"Blues, grays, and blacks," Michael said defensively.

"Then it's possible the thief singled you out because of your skin tones. Then, when he opened your suitcase, he found colors completely different on the color wheel from what he expected. So he decided to return your clothes."

"What is this wheel you keep talking about?" Michael asked.

"Here, Mr. Perry, I'll show you my color wheel," he said, taking it out of his suit pocket. "Here are my colors—which are considered cool colors, in the blue family, especially. See how when I hold this up to my face it complements my skin tones? But now when I hold this color up to your face, it doesn't really do much for you. Here, come and look in the mirror."

Michael looked in the mirror. "I see what you mean. It makes me look terrible." He sounded shocked.

"When I hold up fabric that's warmer, like this dark peach towel, for instance, it brings out that natural glow you have."

Excitedly, Michael said, "It really does."

"If you'd like, Mr. Perry, I know a personal color consultant, Sergio. I could arrange for him to meet with you to do your colors for you."

"That'd be great. I've been thinking that my clothes really don't do much for me. You could set it up for me to meet with him?"

"I'd be happy to, Mr. Perry."

"How soon could you do it?"

"I'll go call him right now."

Armand left.

After the door closed I said in disbelief, "Let me get this right. You, the man who wore a gray shirt, brown pants, black shoes, and blue socks to our engagement dinner, are going to have a personal color consultation with some guy named Sergio?"

"Why not?"

"It's just never been your style before now. I've picked out most of your clothes since we've been married. I always thought they looked good on you."

"Honey," Michael asked, "why do you always have to take everything so personally?"

4

The Mom Who Made a Scrapbook So Large She Could Only Get It Downstairs by Hiring Professional Piano Movers

One day over coffee at Starbucks, one of the moms said, "Well, I finished archiving my latest memory book on my youngest child's first Happy Meal at McDonald's." A murmur of admiration rose from the table.

I innocently asked, "What are you talking about?"

They all looked shocked.

I said, "What's wrong?"

The mom I knew the best said, "Archiving a memory book. You know—scrapbooking—where you take your photos and dress them up by putting buttons, cutouts of leaves, and all kinds of fun things on pages to commemorate a special event."

I said, "I know, but what does that have to do with a Happy Meal at McDonald's?"

They all looked at the floor. I retorted, "What?"

Another mom explained, "Well, a child's first Happy Meal is a very special event."

I said, "Yes, but only to the heirs of Ray Kroc, the guy who started McDonald's."

Another mom said boldly, "Do you mean to say that you don't have at least one scrapbook page detailing Caroline's first trip to McDonalds?"

Something inside me told me to run, but I foolishly passed up this little piece of intuitive advice.

"No," I said. "I had never even considered it."

They all gasped.

After coffee, I went straight home. About twenty minutes later, another mom, Jane, called and said, "I just got word that you have never archived Caroline's first Happy Meal at McDonald's into a scrapbook. And I'm calling to offer my support."

"Support?" I asked.

"Well, someone is going to have to take charge of archiving Caroline's encounters with fast food and it might as well be me. Why don't you come over Friday evening and join us for a cropping session? You'll have fun," she encouraged.

"Cropping?" I asked.

"That's what we call it when we archive pictures of a special event onto vellum or other nonporous paper."

I had no idea what she had just said, but thought I might check it out.

When I pulled up to Jane's house, I couldn't find a park-

ing space closer than six blocks away. I thought that someone must be having quite a party.

Approaching the house, I noticed the garage doors were
open. The cars had been removed and six long tables had
been set up, which were already packed with women poring
over their scrapbooks. Strategically placed throughout the
garage were propane heaters. Japanese lanterns had been
hung from the ceiling.

Jane walked up to me. "Welcome!" she gushed. "I should
have told you to come earlier. All the spaces have already
been filled."

I stood stunned.

"I thought seventy-two spaces for working on memory
books would be enough," Jane continued, "but I was wrong.
I'd be happy to put you on the waiting list. Why don't you come
in? Let me show you some of my favorite scrapbooks."

She led me into the house. In the living room, the furniture had been removed and replaced with a large table, with no
chairs. In the dining room, there was also a table, again with
no chairs.

She caught my glance and knew I was wondering why she
had such an unusual setup in her house. She said, "I perma-
nently removed all the furniture and added another table
so that I would have a place to display some of my favorite
scrapbooks."

On each of the tables sat eight scrapbooks, where you
would normally see china settings. Track lighting had been
installed to illuminate each scrapbook. The music playing
in the background was Rod Stewart's "Every Picture Tells a
Story."

"I had mahogany stands built to raise each of the books for better viewing," Jane said proudly.

"Oh, really," I said, feeling a little uneasy.

"The table in the living room contains scrapbooks chronicling 1995 to 1999. The dining-room table chronicles 2000 to 2005."

I ventured to open a scrapbook labeled 2003. I turned to a page entitled, TRIPS TO TARGET. Her three girls were posed outside the store, and each wore red-and-white clothing that matched the Target sign.

I said weakly, "I think I need to sit down."

She smiled. "Everyone on the waiting list is sitting out back drinking margaritas."

"Perfect," I replied. At least the evening wouldn't be a complete waste of time.

I went out back and sat down next to a mom I had seen around school.

"So," she said, "I understand that you're the one that needs help."

"That's true on many levels."

"Would you like to see the photos I'm planning for my scrapbook?"

I nodded.

She said proudly, "These are photos of my summer shoe collection."

"Your summer shoe collection?"

"Yes," she said. "I thought that I had put everything I could think of into a scrapbook, and then at the seminar I attended, someone suggested a scrapbook of summer shoes. I will be archiving them into ten different categories:

1. Dressy sandals (the white collection),
2. Dressy sandals (the color collection),
3. Casual sandals (white and colored combined),
4. Casual athletic shoes that look good,
5. Casual one-inch heels,
6. Dressy one-inch heels,
7. Open-toe two-inch-heel sling-backs,
8. Pointed-toe two-inch-heel sling-backs,
9. Closed-toe two-inch-heel pumps, and
10. Pointed-toe two-inch-heel pumps."

In response to this little piece of information, I finished off my margarita and went to see if I could find any hard liquor. After I luckily found some gin in the kitchen, Jane grabbed me by the arm. "I'm so sorry you have to wait for a spot to get started. By my calculations, a place at table four should be opening up around three a.m."

"Three a.m.?" I cried, perplexed.

"Oh, didn't I tell you? We're going to be cropping around the clock for the next seventy-two hours. You did arrange for someone to take Caroline to school on Monday morning, didn't you?"

"People are going to be cropping until *when*?"

"Monday, of course. Oh, you haven't seen my latest creation." She pulled me upstairs. "Are you ready for this?"

"No, I'm quite sure that I am not ready for this."

"Silly," she laughed. "And now . . . my latest scrapbook."

She pronounced the last three words in a hushed voice filled with reverence.

Ushering me into the upstairs hallway, she said, "This is the best scrapbook that I have ever archived. I have it sitting here on this table in the hall. The scrapbook is so heavy that I had to stack concrete blocks under the table; otherwise it starts to sag."

"The table starts to sag?" I said incredulously.

"The problem is that I want to move the scrapbook downstairs to the family room, but it's too heavy. I have scheduled piano movers to move it, but first we need to reinforce one of the floor beams under the family room. Two hydraulic jacks should do it."

"Oh," I said, feeling numb. "It looks great."

We went back downstairs and she turned to me, "Now, tell me what you'd like to start cropping. You could perhaps start with something the size of the book I just showed you, or bigger. What weight of paper would you like to use? How about the lettering? What kind of accents, design sketches, mats, journaling, borders, and patterns?"

I downed the gin martini I had thankfully found earlier. Suddenly, I felt inspired. Perhaps I just could scrapbook my favorite liquors. Thinking back to the shoe archiver for inspiration, I thought, "Let's divide martinis into five categories:

1. The chocolate martini (my personal favorite: a dessert and a drink all at once; what could be better?),
2. The sour apple martini (for when I'm feeling feisty),

3. The lemon drop martini (always perfect for summer),

4. The peppermint vodka martini (served during the winter holidays), and

5. The James Bond martini (for drinking and drooling)."

5

The Woman Who Can Plant 145 Petunias Without Referring to Them as "Those Little Bastards" by the Time She Is Finished

My lawn was a mess again this year. I got the hint when someone gave me a book about gardening with small explosives. Well, no more!

The next day, I was out weeding (score: Lauren, 8; weeds, 1,756) when I remembered hearing stories about the Master Gardener in my county—a person who has passed a number of required courses on gardening and can give helpful advice. People spoke of her with reverence, so I thought I'd give her a call.

When I dialed her number, a woman answered tersely, "Garden and Lawn Hotline, is this an emergency?"

I was confused. "Is this the Master Gardener?"

"Yes," she said impatiently. "Is this an emergency?"

"Ah, no. I'm just calling about a spirea bush."

"Is it about to die?" she asked anxiously.

"No, it's just not doing very well."

"I can't deal with vague statements like that," she said irritably. "Get over here as fast as you can. That spirea bush is probably about to die any minute and you don't even know it." She hung up the phone.

When I arrived, she greeted me brusquely, saying, "I need to make a quick call before I can help you. Some idiot called and asked if he could put peat moss on his irises. Everyone *knows* that you can only use organic kelp on irises. I'll be right back. Feel free to look around."

After much scolding of the kelp person, she came back with fifteen different pictures for me to see. They were labeled, SPIREAS IN DISTRESS—HOW TO DIAGNOSE THE PROBLEM AND DELIVER AID QUICKLY.

"Which one of these pictures best describes your spirea?" she asked.

Numbly, I pointed to number seven.

"Oh—my—God," she said, with a dramatic pause between each word. "How could you let that happen?"

"Ah, well, ah, gosh, I don't know."

"Okay," she said briskly. "We're going to need to overhaul your entire backyard. Come in here and we'll get started."

She led me into a room that had been built off her garage. I looked around the room and saw there were computer screens everywhere monitoring different parts of her yard. Included on the screen were data about the pH level of the soil, what fertilizer had been used last, and the humidity in each area of the garden.

She said, "Okay, let's get started. Now I have a question for you. What is the foundation of a garden?"

"What?"

She rolled her eyes. "What is the foundation of a garden?" she said louder.

"Dirt?" I tried.

21

"No," she said irritably. And then loudly and slowly she said: "*Bulbs.*"

"Oh, of course," I said, wondering if I made a run for it if she'd tackle me and hold me down.

"Now," she continued, "what courses have you taken in gardening at both undergraduate and graduate levels?"

I was afraid to answer. "None?" I said hesitantly. I hate to put statements in the form of a question, but in this case I had no other choice.

Suddenly, I heard a strange ringing.

"That's the red phone!" she shrieked and jumped to answer it.

It was then that I noticed the ominous-looking crimson phone, which was now lit up and blinking wildly.

She listened on the phone for a few seconds and then asked, "Address?" She jotted down the information. "I'll be right there!"

"Lauren!" she shouted. "I need to go. Some abysmally ignorant fool is about to put down the wrong shade of gray mulch. I've had problems with my garage door, and I need you to help me get it open."

I rushed to help her with the door. We got it open and she jumped into her Hummer.

"That's an unusual color for a vehicle," I commented to her. "I've never seen it before." It was a kind of emerald-aquamarine color.

"I had it custom-ordered," she said. "I wanted my Hummer to match the color of my favorite fertilizer, the 30-10-20."

She glanced over at me. I must have looked afraid.

"Don't be alarmed," she shouted while she backed up. "I've

decided not to use the siren." She squealed her tires and hit the road.

As I drove home, I thought about reading that book on gardening with small explosives. It might feel good to blow something up.

6

The Mom Who Is Happy All the Time and Uses the Word "Golly" Whenever She Can

Caroline and I arrived at the community swimming pool on a weekday morning. She waved and ran over to join her friend Gigi and I followed.

"Are you Caroline's mom?" a pretty, young-looking blond woman asked.

"Maybe," I replied cautiously. I had fallen into this trap before.

"I'm Gigi's mother, Dee Dee. Golly, Caroline, and Gigi were in the same class last year." She giggled happily. "Gee whiz, if you'd like to sit by me, that would be really, really fun!" The girls left to swim.

"Oh, okay," I said, a little taken aback by her unmitigated enthusiasm.

After we talked a bit, I realized I had never met anyone so wide-eyed and enthusiastically surprised by every topic of conversation.

"Golly, Lauren, what's your favorite color?"

"My favorite color?" I said, thinking I hadn't heard her correctly.

She nodded brightly.

"Well, I guess it's black, unless I'm in a very festive mood, and then it's gray."

She giggled, "Golly, Lauren, you're such a kidder. My favorite colors are soft pink, sky blue, and buttercup yellow. Do you have any pets?"

"We have a few cats."

"I've always had dogs. They're just so happy! Their names are Buster and Duster, isn't that cute?"

"Oh, yeah, very cute."

"I've never understood cats. They seem so . . . so . . ." Her voice trailed off.

"So aloof, unapproachable, and detached?"

She just giggled. "Once, when Duster was little, he found a can I had thrown in the garbage, and he got it stuck on his nose! It was so adorable. And another time, the TV remote was on the recliner, and Buster jumped up and sat with his paw on top of the remote, as if he were going to change the channel. Can you believe it?" She quivered with joy.

"Wow."

"Golly, I might have some pictures of them in my purse." She started digging for the photos, while discussing her favorite recipe for chocolate chip cookies and her favorite pop star.

"Golly, Lauren, do you have the latest Jessica Simpson CD?" she asked.

"No, I somehow missed that one."

"Gee whiz, Lauren is such a pretty name; I just love names that start with 'L,'" she said brightly.

I thought about drowning myself, but there were too many lifeguards.

"Golly, I thought I had Buster and Duster's photos with me, but I guess not. Oh, well!" she said.

I had a momentary ray of hope that the conversation would expand a bit when she described her family's vacation cycling across Colorado, but then she ruined it by going into a long monologue about her bicycle outfits.

"Golly, I don't know why it's so hard to find all-pink bicycling outfits. Do you have any idea where I could find some?"

"I'm not the best person to ask."

"Gee whiz, why not?"

"Don't you remember, Dee Dee? My favorite color is black."

"Oh, yeah, I forgot!" she giggled, seemingly embarrassed that she had already forgotten my favorite color.

I asked her if she had had a career before Gigi was born. "Golly, I used to be an aerobics instructor." I thought she might break out into a Jazzercise routine to the tune of "My Favorite Things," but she just giggled and bounced off to the snack bar to get a round of ice-cream cones with sprinkles on top.

A little later, while I was expending some energy of my own by rolling onto my stomach to tan my back, Dee Dee said, "Golly, I guess I'll swim a few laps before we leave. Would you like to join me, Lauren?"

"No, no, you go ahead," I said. "I hate to get wet."

She just giggled.

All this happy energy was sucking the life right out of me.

26

That evening I asked Michael, "Have you ever met Gigi's perky mom? When she talks, she says 'golly' every other word. Really annoying."

He replied that yes, he had met Dee Dee at the pool and thought the "golly" thing was charming.

"You can't tell me that old wide-eyed blond allure is still valid with men?" I snapped.

"Definitely," he retorted.

Galling as it seems, tonight in bed I am going to start saying "golly" to Michael as often as possible. Let's see how alluring it is when *I* say it.

7

The Couple Who Write the Holiday Letter Telling You How Their Little Timmy Came Up with an Alternative to Fossil Fuels

The first example of an annoying holiday letter was written by a couple we know:

Holiday greetings from the Levinson family!

Last year our Ryan finished his college degree, and he's only seven years old. He's planning to graduate medical school and become a brain surgeon by the time he's eleven.

Our daughter, twelve-year-old Rachel Mary-Alice, decided to try out for the diving team at her school. Her coach was so impressed that she immediately signed Rachel Mary-Alice up for the Olympic competitions, and to everyone's shock, she won the gold medal.

Last year our little Timmy (he's nine) developed a cheap, easy alternative to fossil fuels. So far, he has banked about $7 billion from this new way for society to use energy. We are so proud.

And also this last year, our Meagan gave her first solo a cappella performance at Carnegie Hall. She somehow manages to balance voice practice with her nuclear physics coursework at Columbia! Last fall, as you may have seen on television, she was named Miss Universe.

Here's to a New Year full of new achievements!

The second example of an annoying holiday letter came from another couple:

Dear friends and family,

We spent January in Australia, navigating our boat in the World Cup, and we won.

In February, while still in Australia, our friend Nicole Kidman asked us over for lunch; she wanted our opinion on what dress to wear to the Academy Awards.

In March, we flew to Paris after being asked to teach an afternoon cooking class with the world-renowned chef Pierre DuBois. While we were there, the French Prime Minister found out we were in town and invited us to spend the weekend.

Afterward, we decided to spend a few nights at the Ritz. The food was exquisite. We had iced poached shrimp in the shell with pink chaud-froid, consommé brunoise, crown roast of lamb with tangerine-rice dressing cockaigne, cold green beans a la grecque, and fresh fruit with sabayon sauce for dessert.

A highlight of our stay at the Ritz was the visit of Mohamed Al-Fayed, who stopped by and begged us to stay with him at the French chateau Dodi had bought for Diana. He showed us a number of photos of Diana and Dodi's last few weeks together. These candid shots have never been released to the public. Too bad you'll never get to see them—Diana looked fabulous.

In May, Princess Caroline of Monaco asked us to come and spend the month with her. Monaco is so delightful in May. We drove along the Corniche to Cannes and took in some of the film festival as well. After the screening, we had an aperitif with Annette Bening and Warren Beatty at a waterfront café.

In June, we took a private yacht tour through several Norwegian fjords and in July, we attended the fiesta in Pamplona, Spain (made famous by Ernest Hemingway).

During August, we spent much of our time at our estate on Martha's Vineyard. The Trumps begged us to use their yacht as ours was being redecorated with the new Italian marble we had purchased on the way home from Spain.

We spent autumn at our home in the Hamptons. We had our decorations for Christmas put up early since Architectural Digest, Veranda, *and* Town and Country *wanted to shoot photos of our house for their December magazine issues.*

Our Christmas, of course, is usually spent with Diane Sawyer and Mike Nichols. Mike always asks us to read upcoming scripts for him to get our opinion on which movies he should do. While we find this to be a bit tedious, we are happy to help him out.

Here's hoping that your lives are not too boring!

The holiday letters my husband and I send out, sadly, are at the opposite end of the spectrum:

Holiday greetings from the Perrys!

On January 27, we swept the garage floor. There were two dustpans full of dirt, although the second dustpan was only about three-quarters full. We debated whether to use the hose to wash the garage out, but decided against this since the temperature was below freezing.

On February 5, we were thrilled to get a personal call from AT&T wanting us to switch over from MCI. We told them we'd think about it.

We spent the month of March figuring out how many frequent-flier miles we have. We finally determined that we were eligible for a two-for-one coupon for drinks, provided we pay full coach fare.

On April 7, we replaced the light bulb in the family room. It hadn't been replaced since we moved here in 1990.

On May 4, we realized we hadn't emptied the lint in our dryer since we moved here either.

On June 17, we spent the day trying to adjust the color on the television. It was difficult to get it "just right."

On July 7, we bought a new dryer.

On August 15, we went out to eat at Applebee's. We had cheese sticks as an appetizer, and then Michael had the teriyaki chicken salad and Lauren had the chicken fajitas. The lettuce in Michael's salad was on the verge of wilting, but still okay to eat. They brought a dessert tray out, but the carrot cake didn't look like it had enough frosting on it and the chocolate pudding with Cool Whip looked rather dry. The apple dumplings were a possi-bility, but since they weren't willing to warm them up, we decided against dessert.

On September 3, we ordered new checks. Since we live in Colorado, we decided to order ones with mountains in the background. The writing on the checks is done in calligraphy, and the "P" in Perry is larger than all the other letters.

On October 22, Lauren cleaned out her car. In it she found her glasses, fourteen Milk Duds, five unopened prescription medications, and twenty-eight coffee mugs.

On November 24, we discussed buying mint-flavored floss.

On December 3, AT&T called back, wondering what we wanted to do. Since we hate feeling pressured, we told them we'd stay with MCI.

That's it for our year! Here's to another great year!

8

The Husband Who Buys a New Video Camera and Now Believes He's Martin Scorsese

Last year over the holidays I decided I had spent one too many Christmases with my husband and his video camera. I said to him, "Look, you're going to have to *let go* a little bit around this video camera. My family has threatened not to visit for Christmas this year if we have a repeat of last year."

He said, "I don't know what you're talking about."

"Maybe you missed your calling, but sitting around in that director's chair with that baseball cap on and barking orders into a megaphone to what you call the crew—in other words, Uncle Alex and Aunt Mildred—is not what Christmas is all about."

"I can't help it if they know nothing about film production."

"Honey, it's just a family Christmas."

"To you maybe. To me, it's a short film documentary on 'Serious Interpretation of Holiday Celebration Customs in

American Suburban Life at the Beginning of the Twenty-First Century.'"

"Oh, for heaven's sakes," I said. "You're losing it."

"I am not."

"You don't think referring to me as the 'lighting production manager' just because I turned on the lights in the family room is going a bit far?"

"No," he said defensively.

"You throw around phrases like 'it's a wrap' and 'roll it' as if you were making the sequel to *Gone With the Wind*."

"Not true."

"And referring to the cat as an 'extra' is confusing to him. For that matter, it's confusing to all of us. And if you think no one has noticed you're using my makeup pencil to make your eyebrows look more like Martin Scorsese's, you're wrong. And why are you wearing those thick black glasses? You don't even need glasses."

"They make me look more distinguished."

"They make you run into things."

I recognized these early signs in my husband because of my experience with my brother. My brother is the original video dad, which means his entire life since 1979 when the first luggable thirty-pound personal-use video camera became available for four thousand dollars. I stopped going on vacations with his family because I didn't want to carry "my share" of the video equipment around amusement parks or have myself on video trying to get up on water skis. Nor did I want to watch these episodes where every tape had him laughing in the background.

Christmas morning at his house went something like this: "Lauren!" (this shouted). "Pretend to open that sweater again and hold it up. I was taping Alex opening his train set. Come on! Hurry up! Mom's opening her big present next. Hurry!"

How fun.

And then when my husband bought a video camera, the two of them were inseparable. They were both big fans of TV in the sixties and seventies, which meant that for years we had to replicate Christmas from their favorite shows. The *Gilligan's Island* holiday was actually kind of fun with the boat theme and all. Unfortunately, my sister-in-law landed the part of Ginger, while I ended up as Mrs. Howell. And then another year while we were all dividing up the parts for a *Brady Bunch* Christmas, I went to the bathroom, came back, and found that she had taken the part of Carol Brady and I was left playing Alice. And during the *Dick Van Dyke Show* holiday, she got to be Laura Petrie and I had to play Millie. It seemed to be a trend.

Before the holidays this past year, I said to Michael, "This year, I think we should not do the theme thing. Let's just have a normal holiday."

"But honey," Michael replied. "Your brother and I have it all planned. We're doing a *Cheers* holidays celebration this year."

I said cautiously, "An old *Cheers* or a newer *Cheers*?"

"A newer *Cheers*."

"Fine," I said. "I get to play Kirstie Alley's part."

"Sorry, hon," he said. "That part is already taken. You can be either Carla or Cliff."

"Fine," I shouted, "I'll be Cliff."

A cross-dressing role should really be a boost to my acting career.

9

The Perfect Soccer Mom Who Knows All the International Rules of Soccer

Unfortunately, Caroline's soccer organization requires parents to volunteer as part of the whole soccer experience. And since I forgot to check the volunteer sign-up sheet early enough online, all the good volunteer positions were already taken, such as buying a whistle for the coach, or making a one-time orange juice drop-off. Disappointingly, all that was left was the position of assistant coach.

"But I don't know anything about soccer," I whined to the volunteer coordinator.

"You'll be fine," she said. "You'll be coaching with Karen, and she attended UCLA on a soccer scholarship."

The day of our first game was bright and sunny, unfortunately. I'd secretly hoped we'd get rained out. The phone rang early that morning and it was Karen. "Lauren, you'll have to go on without me. I have a 103-degree temperature and have been sick all night. The referee that will be there today seems very stern, but don't let him scare you. I'm sure you'll be fine."

How hard could it be?

The beginning of the game went well. No goals, but everyone played well. In the second half, I was busy talking with another mom when the referee's whistle caught my attention. He called a foul on one of my girls.

"Wait, what's going on?" I hollered at the referee. "What did she do?"

"She was offside," he shouted.

I ran out on the field. "What do you mean she was offside?"

He said, "She was nearer to her opponents' goal line than both the ball and the second-last opponent."

"What do you mean, 'second-last opponent'? Does that have anything to do with birth order? I know birth order is important, but I don't really know what it has to do with soccer."

He looked confused.

"Plus," I continued. "You said Amanda was offside and she's an only child. So I think you are mistaken about this whole thing."

"Look," he said impatiently. "Being offside doesn't have anything to do with birth order. Let me explain it to you. A player is not offside if she is level with the second-last opponent or she is level with the last two opponents."

I was silent for a minute. "So if Amanda were level with the second-last opponent or with the last two opponents, she wouldn't be offside?" I asked.

He nodded, looking relieved.

I said, "But Amanda is taller than Rachel, but shorter than Kelsie. So I don't know how she could be level with them."

He shook his head. "No, no, no, no, no."

"Girls, come over here and show the referee how tall you are." I had the girls line up in descending order.

"Really, ma'am, trust me, she was offside."

One of my girls said, "Really, Mrs. Perry, she was offside."

"Well, if you think so . . ." My voice trailed off and I walked back to my lawn chair.

As I was continuing my conversation with the other mom, that irritating whistle blew again.

He yelled, "Throw-in penalty."

I ran over to him again and asked, "What did you say is wrong now?"

"It's a throw-in penalty."

"How can that be? Throwing in is throwing in. She threw the ball in." I didn't understand.

"What happened to the coach who played at UCLA?"

"She's sick. I'm the assistant coach."

He swore softly to himself.

Then he said irritatingly, "The ball must be thrown from behind and over her head."

"But it's the second half and all the girls are tired," I said. "No one could be expected to raise their arms all the way over their head while holding a ball. It's asking too much."

"That's the rule."

"Don't be ridiculous. Who would ever come up with a picky rule like that?"

He replied curtly, "The International Soccer Association."

Obviously, it was a sore subject, so I went back to my lawn chair.

The next time the whistle blew, I automatically began to rise from my chair.

"Stay where you are," he yelled. "It's a rule. *Trust me.* I've been a referee for twenty years." I sat back down and there was a collective sigh of relief from my players. Miraculously, we won the game.

Karen, the other coach, called the next day and congratulated me on the win. I confided, "You know, I'm not sure if these referees know what they're doing."

Karen laughed and said, "From what I heard, it sounds like you were really on top of things and didn't let anything get by. I'm sure that referee never had anyone question him on anything before."

"Oh, well, thanks. I'll see you at practice."

I was feeling pretty good about the whole thing. As I went off to take a nap, I wondered if I was too old for a soccer scholarship to UCLA. After all, I know all those ridiculously elaborate rules now. That has to be the hardest part.

10

The Mom Who Corrects the Grammar of the Policeman Who Pulled Her Over for Speeding

In front of the school one morning, I ran into the Grammar Mom. My daughter was to be visiting her daughter that afternoon.

"What time shall I pick up Caroline?" I inquired.

"Oh, around five o'clock," she replied. "At seven I'm giving a two-hour speech at the Grammarians of Denver meeting."

I had heard rumors of the Grammar Mom, but I had never realized the extent of her commitment to grammar.

She went on, "I'll be discussing the improper use of the word 'like' instead of 'as.' Mixing metaphors and similes is outrageous."

"Yes," I replied, "it's just beyond belief," even though I was uncertain as to what she had just said.

"Well, really. What's more important than one's grammar?"

My mind flashed on world peace, a reduction in global warming, and an end to hunger and disease.

She ranted on. "Adjectives substituted for adverbs, subjective and objective pronouns mixed—it's simply criminal."

Thanking God for the grammar feature on my computer, I went home.

⁓⁓⁓⁓⁓

At five o'clock I drove over to pick up Caroline. As the Grammar Mom went to call the girls, I entered the living room. On the walls, I noticed some new-looking artwork in blueprint-blue with white lines. *Très chic!*

"Are you having some blueprints done for a new addition or something?" I asked when she returned. "These look beautiful."

"Aren't they wonderful!" she exclaimed. "Thank you for noticing them. We had an artist do color renderings of three of our favorite diagrammed sentences."

I began to stare intently at her.

"See, it's abstract," she said, "but if you look closely, you can see where the subject and predicate split." She stepped up next to me. I could feel her excitement level rising. "And over here you can see the prepositional clause moves off at this angle. I believe one's artwork should reflect one's loves and values, don't you agree?"

Verbally paralyzed by the fear of making a grammatical *faux pas,* I loudly blurted out, "Okay."

She smiled. "Diagramming sentences has always been a little hobby of mine. I feel the alphabet is similar to molecular biology: the very building blocks of our lives. It has to be the next great science."

I murmured, "It seems you've been devoted to grammar for a long time."

"Oh, heavens, yes! I've been 'into' grammar since I was quite young. And my sisters have always enjoyed it when

I've corrected their grammar. Whenever they send me letters, I send them back with the grammar corrected in red ink. A few months ago, when we all got together, they fondly referred to me as the 'Grammar Bitch.' Isn't that darling?"

"Cute." I tried to sound believable.

"And when I met my husband, it was love at first sight," the Grammar Mom continued. "He's a well-known lexicographer."

I was clueless.

"You know," she prompted, "a person who compiles dictionaries."

I nodded, bleakly.

Just then our daughters ran in.

"Grammar's really fun, Mom," my daughter said. "You know how you taught me to respond with 'This is she' when someone asks for me on the phone? Well, you were actually right!"

A verbal miracle, I thought.

"Yes, I was impressed." The Grammar Mom gave me a conspiratorial smile. I guess we "Grammar Bitches" have to stick together.

"Wasn't it Mrs. Whitehead, your teacher, who taught you that?" I asked my daughter.

The Grammar Mom snorted. "Mrs. Whitehead wouldn't know a dependent clause from a dangling participle. That's why my daughter goes to Grammar Camp every summer. Perhaps Caroline would like to attend . . . also." She had a certain way of pausing where a comma should be and it was driving me crazy.

Her daughter exclaimed, "Oh, please, could she? Last year we had a contest to see who could list the most superlative adverbs, and I won, and we slept in tents and this year I want to—"

"Stephanie! You're speaking a run-on sentence!" the Grammar Mom exclaimed.

I thought back, remembering all the times I had used a run-on sentence that day.

As we left, the Grammar Mom called down the walk, "Remember, a preposition is not a word to end a sentence *with*!"

The three of them laughed. Apparently a little grammar humor. Caroline explained the joke to me on the way home.

Within a mile of our house, a policeman pulled me over for speeding. I guess I'd been preoccupied thinking about the Grammar Mom. He took my license and registration and returned again in a few minutes.

"I'll just give you a warning, ma'am," he said politely. "Please slow down, and drive safe."

My experience with the Grammar Mom had emboldened me. I said, "You mean, safe*ly*."

"My name isn't Lee," he said, perplexed.

"No, I meant you should have said, 'Drive safe*ly*.' It's very important to use correct grammar." Converting him actually felt pretty good.

He shook his head and wandered off.

I looked at my watch. I'd still have time to get to that seven o'clock Grammarians of Denver meeting.

11

The Woman Who Decorates Her Yard for Columbus Day Using Replicas of the *Niña,* the *Pinta,* and the *Santa María*

Little did I realize how substandard I was in the category of exterior holiday decoration until last year, when we moved to a new neighborhood and I encountered the Holiday Decorating Woman. Several days after moving in I was walking the dog when I came upon her house and yard.

As I approached, I saw a wax statue of Martin Luther King, Jr., at a podium. Behind him was a mural of a crowd at the Reflecting Pool from the National Mall in Washington, D.C.

A small sign read, PLEASE PRESS BUTTON, and I couldn't resist.

Suddenly, a loudspeaker began spewing excerpts from the "I Have A Dream" speech followed by the voice of Charlton Heston narrating highlights of Dr. King's life.

Stunned, I stumbled home to consult my next-door neighbor, Sue. She said, "Oh, that's just Beverly. Today is Martin Luther King's birthday. This town's big on outdoor decorating. Beverly always wins the top prize. Sometimes she stays up all night putting up decorations."

"Is there a monetary prize for outdoor decorations?"

"No, it's pride of accomplishment," Sue sniffed.

"Oh, cool," I said, backing away.

During the second week in February, there was a wax figure of Lincoln giving his speech at Gettysburg. The side yard depicted Mary Todd Lincoln having a nervous breakdown back at the White House. I asked Sue if it was the display for Presidents' Day.

"Oh, I'm sure not," she chuckled. "That's just for Lincoln's Birthday."

Sure enough, on February 22 the Holiday Decorating Woman had a model of Mount Vernon on the front lawn, including a live mule like the one Washington received from the King of Spain for his birthday. Unfortunately, the mule ate all the dogwoods she had flown in for the day.

On March 30, there appeared a life-size statue of Secretary of State Seward shaking hands with the Czar of Russia for the anniversary of the United States's purchase of Alaska. Upon closer inspection, though, I did think that the czar could have been a warmed-over Abe Lincoln.

May 1 featured real actors depicting Flora, the Roman goddess of spring, and her entourage dancing around the maypole. I was hoping they'd expand the dancing into some exotic pagan rituals, but it never happened.

On May 11, I was surprised to see a sign proclaiming, in both French and English, that it was Joan of Arc Day. The display could only be termed gruesome.

"This is getting ridiculous," I said to my husband one

evening. "The whole town is totally engrossed in this. Yesterday, I couldn't even get into our garage because it was so crowded at Beverly's."

"You're just jealous because you've never even hung a string of lights outdoors," he replied. He had a point.

I couldn't take my daily walk on the Fourth of July because the exhaust from all the cars driving by made my dog cough too much.

On Columbus Day, fog softly wafted around her yard. In the haze were eighteen-foot replicas of the *Niña,* the *Pinta,* and the *Santa María,* in a geographically correct position, sailing from Spain to the Bahamas. On the east side of the yard Spaniards waved good-bye and on the west side unsuspecting Native Americans ate the last peaceful ears of corn they would ever enjoy.

Several holidays *were* culturally enriching, though. For example, neither my husband nor I knew that October 24 is United Nations Day. This featured about three hundred national flags, and a Henry Kissinger impersonator chatting amongst the neighbors and letting them kiss his ring.

And then, sadly, one day, my lights flickered off and on followed by a booming sound outside. When I went out to check, I saw a cloud of smoke billowing up from the Holiday Decorating Woman's backyard. The Quonset hut where all of her exterior illumination electrical lines came together had blown up. No one was hurt, thank goodness.

Later that day Sue called and said it was all over. She said she had thought about taking up a collection for the $275,000 it would take to replace all the equipment. But then Sue reported that the Holiday Decorating Woman had decided to take a job consulting for Doris Kearns Goodwin on her first coffee table book: *How to Make History Come Alive Through the Use of Exterior Decorations.*

It sounds kind of like a Doris-meets-Martha deal. We should have seen it coming.

12

The Wife Who Actually Knows How to Operate Her Victoria's Secret Lingerie

After purchasing a new little black dress for an upcoming party, I decided to splurge on something better than white cotton underwear. So I set out for a Victoria's Secret store at my favorite mall. I had passed it many times, but could never picture myself in leopard print.

Entering the store was like entering another world. Various shades of pink everywhere, including pink padded hangers. Large gold-framed mirrors hung in convenient spots. Classical music played softly. "I'll bet Mozart had this kind of place in mind when he wrote his Concerto #20," I reflected.

A sleek Rachel Hunter–type salesclerk approached me. She had a measuring tape draped around her neck, which I hoped she didn't feel the need to use on everyone.

"May I help you find something special?" she inquired.

"Well, yes. I was thinking about those black lace undies in your ad in this month's *Vogue*."

"Undies?" She disdainfully pronounced the word as if it were an unfamiliar foreign verb.

"Ah, yes, the black lace undies in the *Vogue* ad," I explained.

"Undies?" She stared at me, pretending not to comprehend.

"Well, that's what we used to call them back home," I said. Didn't she speak English? "It's short for underwear," I explained.

"Sounds romantic," she commented. "Here at Victoria's Secret we don't refer to it as underwear, we refer to it as lingerie."

And then, after sweepingly spreading out her arms to encompass the entire store, she exclaimed, "And it isn't just lingerie, it's a lifestyle."

As I walked into the dressing room to try on some twenty different bras, I quickly realized that I needed to be smarter than the lingerie to get into it. The front-hook bras were a special challenge. You had to put those on like you would a coat; after three tries, I still couldn't do it. When I finally did manage to hook one of them, it must have been too tight because when I unhooked it, it propelled me backward into the pink wall.

Finally, I decided on some of my new lifestyle and made my way to the counter. Another toothpick of a clerk intercepted me. "Do you need any stockings?" she said with a French accent.

I said, "Where are you from?"

"Tulsa," she said, shrugging. "The stockings?"

I thought back to the last pair my dog had chewed up. "Thank you, yes."

One type was particularly intriguing: long sheer stockings that had only wide black stretch lace bands at the top. I purchased them.

I couldn't wait to show them off to Michael. Of course, he was interested in them only from an engineering standpoint.

Several weeks later, I donned the black-lace-banded stockings for an evening at a restaurant with friends. Things were fine during the evening as I sat there crossing and uncrossing my legs.

As we all rose to leave, I felt the stockings loosen. As I crossed the room on Michael's arm, I whispered, "Slow down! I think my stockings are falling down."

"What? Those engineering marvels with the lace tops?"

"Yes!" I hissed, smiling for all I was worth.

"Then shouldn't we speed up?"

"No! I have trapped the tops together with my upper thighs. All I have to do is make it out of here by walking with my knees plastered together." Thank heavens I hadn't lost any leg fat recently.

"I wish you wouldn't do stuff like this," he said under his breath, smiling to the others.

"Stuff like what?" I whispered loudly.

He whispered back. "You are in over your head with all this sexy underwear. Last night you had the thin straps of that low-cut lace nightgown wrapped around your neck and I didn't sleep all night because I was worried you were going to stop breathing." He painted a bleak picture.

"It isn't underwear—it's lingerie. And it isn't just lingerie, it's a lifestyle," I shouted.

All heads turned our way. We both smiled at everyone, and I continued to quickly shuffle inch by inch to the door.

We got into the car and sped away. After about six blocks, Michael pulled over to the curb and I catapulted the stockings out of the window into a garbage can. You can only do so much.

13

The Husband Who Believes You Can't Paint Over Wood

A man can run several companies at once, travel all over the world on business, and remember dates and people with no problem. But when he walks in the door after work, scientific studies cited in the *Journal of Brain Structure* have shown that the male brain structure changes into the husband brain structure.

This is how it works: studies have shown that putting a tight wedding band on a man's ring finger cuts off blood to areas of his brain. However, the components of the husband brain structure only come out in the presence of his wife, and not in the presence of anyone else. In that respect, it is devious.

One component of the husband brain structure is the inability to paint over wood. For example, my husband says to me: "You're not going to paint that nightstand, are you?"

Then I say, "Well, it looks terrible the way it is now."

He says, "But it's wood. You don't paint over wood."

"Well, what difference does that make?"

And he says, "Well, you don't paint over wood. It's an unspoken agreement which has been passed down from generation to generation that you don't paint over wood."

And I say, "I've never heard of that before in my life."

And he says, "Well, you don't paint over wood."

There is no event in his family history that traumatized him, causing him to repeat the sentence "You don't paint over wood." Therefore, it is part of the husband brain structure.

The theory stated in the _Journal of Brain Structure_ is that during the twelveth through the fifteenth centuries (otherwise known as the Dark Ages, when painting over wood was frowned upon), the husband brain structure became firmly ensconced. Wives, however, have the kind of brain structure that has progressed to a level where we can now visualize how something would look painted virtually any color, including the bay leaf green that I have upstairs in the hall.

But husbands have simply never developed this ability, and for hundreds of years now have instead repeatedly mumbled the statement "You don't paint over wood." When asked to explain, they will tell you they aren't even sure what this means anymore.

Another component of the husband brain structure is the tendency not to notice when the furniture you bought shortly after you were married seventeen years ago has started to look shabby.

All you need to do to witness this behavior is to go to a furniture store. You can pick out a couple, any couple, and can hear the wife saying, "I think that hutch would look good in our dining room."

Her husband will reply, "I don't know what's wrong with the hutch we have now."

She will then reply, "The 'hutch' we have is a couple of crates with a board across it, and I've been waiting for the past fifteen years to buy a decent piece of furniture instead of that."

Then he replies, "Well, all of our beer mugs fit just fine on it and they're easy to get to since I don't have to open any doors."

The way she copes with this statement is to walk away from him and pretend she's not really married, and eventually he wanders away to find a TV with a game on.

This inability to notice what is tacky also includes not being able to recognize that what used to be shag carpeting throughout your entire house is now completely flat. He will, however, notice if your television/sound system/computer wasn't manufactured within the last seventy-two hours.

(Authors' note: Many men believe that the wife brain structure also exists in the presence of husbands, but since we are the ones writing this book and we are women, we are under no obligation to explore this possibility any further. We will say that thus far, the *Journal of Brain Structure* offers no research to support the idea of a wife brain structure. We do admit, however, that this research has been conducted and paid for solely by women.)

14

The Woman Who Cleans Out Her Refrigerator Every Thursday Whether It Smells or Not

The contrast between the Woman Who Cleans Out Her Refrigerator Every Thursday Whether It Smells or Not and myself is stark. She has Black and Decker handheld vacuums stationed every five feet in the house. Never is there an unsqueegeed shower, or an unvacuumed floor. Her bed is made even when she's sleeping in it. She crawls up and cleans the gutters around the roof herself. She unscrews and cleans the heating and cooling registers every week. She flips her mattresses once a month. I, of course, do none of these things although I did make the bed one day last week.

The Woman Who Cleans Out Her Refrigerator Every Thursday wears a wraparound Velcro belt that holds a water bottle, sunscreen, safety kit, bottle opener, and tweezers (in case someone walks barefoot on a wood deck). (That is, a *neighbor's* wood deck. *Her* wood deck would never have splinters.) Her kids wear shoes that are multipurpose—rain, snow, shine, hiking, kayaking, pool—shoes that work in any type of activity or weather. By contrast, for four years my daughter wouldn't wear anything but sparkling ruby-red slippers, which she wore hiking, to T-ball games, and to the pool.

Her car is spotless. Her drink holders are never filled with half-finished Diet Cokes. Junior Mints are never stuck to the armrest in the backseat. And no popcorn clings to her black wool skirt when she gets out of the car. But in *my* car, you never go hungry. For instance, while driving one day on my way to work, I remembered that I hadn't eaten and was able to scrounge up something indefinable for breakfast off the floor.

On another occasion, I was on my way to a party and realized I had forgotten to bring a dessert. Not only was I able to scrounge up several dozen cellophane-wrapped mints from the bottom of my purse, but I also found a plate in the trunk of my car from a previous party. It all worked out pretty well.

She also outdoes me at parties by bringing the perfect bottle of wine, like an exquisite merlot that has aged to perfection. On the other hand, last weekend I took wine to a party, and as we were walking up to the door, I looked at the bottle and noticed that its vintage was "last Tuesday."

But it really wouldn't be news to any of my neighbors that I'm not up to the standards of the Woman Who Cleans Out Her Refrigerator Every Thursday Whether It Smells or Not. My husband was standing out on our deck the other day and several of the neighbors were out in their own backyards.

I was in the kitchen and he yelled to me, "You know, since you cleaned off the grill, I haven't been getting the runs like I used to."

I just stood in the kitchen with a towel over my head. Thanks, sweetheart.

15

The Knitting Mom Who Breaks Down and Confesses, "It's Just Like Drugs, But It's Yarn"

I first glimpsed the Knitting Mom at the community swimming pool. I didn't know her, but she and her four daughters were all decked out in identical, adorable cotton-knit two-piece bathing suits, yellow with a daisy theme, which would probably cost ninety dollars each at one of those mother-daughter boutiques.

My next encounter with the Knitting Mom was at a fall soccer game at school. Caroline and one of the Knitting Mom's daughters were playing in the game, but the other three daughters were all wearing gorgeous sweaters. Subtly sneaking closer, I could see that the fronts of their sweaters depicted all the known completed panels of Monet's water lily paintings.

Later that fall, I picked up Caroline from a Girl Scouts meeting. The troop leader asked if I could take Annie, one of the "Monet sweater" girls, home. I said sure.

Annie got into the car. She was wearing a darling little red-and-green hat shaped like a strawberry. I suppressed the urge to scream, "Where did you get that hat!" Instead I casually remarked, "That's a cute hat, Annie. Where did your mom buy it?"

"She didn't. My mom knits and sews all my clothes, including my hats. Same with my sisters, and my daddy, too."

I instantly and overwhelmingly disliked Annie's mother.

Of course, after Annie had been dropped off, Caroline posed the dreaded question.

"Could you knit a strawberry hat for me, Mom?"

"I don't know how to knit, sweetheart."

"You could learn, couldn't you?"

A wave of guilt washed over me.

"Well, of course I can," I said.

I blamed my mother for not teaching me how to knit. But I wasn't above faking it. When in doubt, hire it done.

After consulting the Yellow Pages, I sallied forth with my charge cards to the closest yarn shop.

"We have beginning classes. They run for six weeks," the head knitter explained.

"Actually, I just want to commission you to knit one of those little strawberry hats. Maybe in pink in time for Valentine's Day."

"We could, but there're lots of people ahead of you. Mostly mothers trying to *pass*."

A group of women knitting at a round table in the corner snickered.

"Trying to *pass*?" I asked.

"Yes, mothers and grandmothers trying to pass as knitters. The peer pressure, you know. They mistakenly think that if their child or grandchild has a couple of hand-knit articles, they themselves will look like real knitters."

"I wasn't trying to pass," I stammered. "I just want a hat for my daughter."

More snickering from the corner group.

I adeptly lied. "Besides, I really don't think my doctor would let me knit since I broke my wrist in two places while competing in a world alpine skiing event. Today's the first day I've had my wrist brace off. Just one little hat would do it."

She eyed me suspiciously. "That'll be $39.95 plus five dollars extra for a HAND-KNITTED BY MOM label."

I thought, "$44.95 for one child's hat—she must be out of her mind!" I said, "That's all? Great!" I handed over the money and blew out of there.

Outraged, I sat and seethed in my car. I would show them. I was not going to be treated this way by a bunch of knitters.

The pink hat was ready before Valentine's Day and I sent my husband to pick it up.

"Were the three witches from *Macbeth* knitting over in the corner?" I asked when he returned.

"No, the shop was empty. They were just opening," he replied.

Good! I would know when to go if I had to sneak back.

Unfortunately, Caroline and Annie, the Monet sweater girl, became friends. This meant that I was forced into getting to know her mother. After I drove up to her house to pick up Caroline one afternoon, I squared my shoulders and bravely marched to the front door.

Annie's mom answered the door, needles in hand. The front of her sweater depicted Botticelli's *Birth of Venus*. The colors were just as delicate and lovely as those of the original painting. I wanted to cry.

After a few minutes of chatting, she turned to me hesitantly. "I was wondering if you'd mind if I asked you a question."

I agreed.

"Do you ever feel it's an addiction?"

"Is what an addiction?" I replied.

"Knitting!" she cried. "I wouldn't bring it up, but I see that you're a knitter too. I peeked at Caroline's hat after she hung it up and saw the HAND-KNITTED BY MOM label."

"That was . . . you know, it was, ah . . ." My voice trailed off.

"I'm just afraid I'm over the top," she went on. "It started out as just a harmless pastime when I was having my first child, but now, ten years later . . . let me show you."

I followed her to a large addition on the back of her house. She said, "Through here is my walk-in refrigerator where I store my yarns. Of course they have to stay at thirty-seven degrees."

"Well, naturally," I said, as if I had been refrigerating yarn for years. There was clearly a whole lot more to this knitting thing than I had ever guessed. "And so you feel you may be addicted to knitting?"

"I love to knit, don't you?" she replied joyfully. "But," her face fell slightly, "as my knitting friend Judy always says, 'It's just like drugs, but it's yarn.'"

Stifling a shriek of laughter, I tried to process this analogy to substance abuse. I could imagine treatment centers asking, "Tell me all the substances to which you are addicted: (1) alcohol, (2) cocaine, (3) marijuana, (4) methamphetamines, (5) heroin, and (6) yarn."

"Maybe there's a 'Knitters Anonymous' program you can join. I don't know much about addictions (except food of course), but I'll do my best to help you find one."

"No," the knitter said warily, "I had a bad experience with a Knitters Anonymous club. We had ordered a container-load of wool shipped directly from New Zealand to see if we could open it up, feel it, and then send it back again. A street fight broke out when it was unloaded. Knitters have a very dark side, I've discovered.

"What I really live for," the knitter added, beginning to expound the joys of her obsession, "is the big sheep and yarn festival in Scotland in May. I go every year. What worries me is that my oldest daughter is displaying a serious interest in it. I see all the signs. She goes into the cooler to touch the wool and talks wistfully about her favorite wool weight. So far, I've kept her satisfied with a small crocheting project, but it's only a matter of time. I just cringe at the thought of her clutching some giant size-11 circular needles while obsessing over a king-size afghan." She mentally floated off again. "Maybe something like the Muir Woods California redwoods. A watercolor feel."

The girls came running in and she regained consciousness. I silently thanked my mother for keeping me away from yarn. But if this woman's daughter had the gene for knitting, it was only a matter of time.

I only hope Betty Ford will accept knitters by then.

16

The Infomercial Couple Who Start Every Sentence with "But Wait! There's More!"

While watching infomercials is a way for couples to purchase items without leaving the comfort of their homes, it can go too far.

For example, our friends Marlene and Dave have turned into an infomercial couple. The other evening, while Michael and I were at their house for dinner, instead of discussing their favorite biographies or the latest movies they've seen, they simply repeated phrases like, "But wait, there's more!" or "Keep your cash from ending up in the trash!"

We were no more than through their front door when Dave began telling us about their latest purchase, the Unbelievable Chopper. He had set up a folding table in the living room to give us a demonstration, and the dining-room chairs had been placed strategically around the table in a theater-like fashion. He donned a chef's hat and placed a peach pit in the container.

As if he were addressing a large audience, his voice

boomed, "Because of the amazing 750 megawatts of power, the Unbelievable Chopper will chop this peach pit into a fine dust." He pressed the button, we listened to the 750 megawatts of power whirl around, and then he exclaimed, "*Voila!*" He poured the finely granulated peach pit powder on the table in front of us.

Michael began to cough. I said to Dave, "I think Michael is allergic to peach pit dust."

Dave said irritably, "You're missing the point."

I said, "No, I think it's fabulous that the Unbelievable Chopper will make peach pit dust."

He said triumphantly, "That's because of the 750 megawatts of power."

I wondered how "mega" power was different from regular power, but didn't want to sit through the explanation.

Michael stopped coughing. He said, "What do you use peach pit dust for?"

Dave said, "You don't use peach pit dust for anything. I'm just trying to prove a point. Now look. I'm going to place these pieces of concrete into the Unbelievable Chopper and it will turn them into a fine sand."

He hit the button and poured out the concrete dust. Michael started coughing again.

"Good heavens," said Dave, "are you allergic to everything?"

I suggested, "Perhaps the Colorado Department of Transportation could use one of these to remove an old highway."

"You are missing the point," Dave said irritably. "The Unbelievable Chopper is for chopping kitchen items."

I said, "Like old forks and spoons?"

"No," he shouted, "like tomatoes and mushrooms."

Marlene walked into the room. "Are you done showing them the Unbelievable Chopper? Because I want to show them my abs." She lifted up her shirt to reveal perfectly toned abs.

Michael coughed again. I knew it wasn't the allergies this time.

She said, "I got these abs with the Smart Stomach Machine. Just two minutes a day for two weeks. But wait, there's more! I don't have to go to the gym now, the gym comes to me!"

Michael and I both nodded numbly.

Weeks later, when I stopped by Marlene's house, I noticed the Smart Stomach Machine sitting out on their curb for the garbage truck.

As we sat down to coffee I said, "It's too bad the Smart Stomach Machine didn't work out. Why are you getting rid of it? Your abs look great."

"I didn't have room for it."

"But your abs look great," I insisted.

She waved me aside. "I stopped eating banana splits every night." Then she hesitated and said, "You know, I'm beginning to realize that infomercials are running our lives. I haven't ordered anything for a whole month. But I'll tell you who I'm worried about, it's Dave."

"Why?"

"He's never been able to resist any salesperson. Did you notice the statues all over our lawn? There's a new statuary place on his way to work. They have placed signs every hundred feet before the store, and he just becomes mesmerized and pulls in. Lately I've had to drive him to and from work, blindfolded, so he can't see the signs. It's getting to be a problem."

I would agree that having to drive your husband to and from work blindfolded would qualify as a problem.

She went on. "I didn't mind so much at first. He brought home statues of bunnies and a nice little fountain. But now he just buys anything they have. And frankly, I don't like going into my backyard and seeing a fifty-foot statue of an alligator. I just can't relax out there anymore."

I glanced out the window at the backyard. It looked like a scene from *Crocodile Hunter*. I said, "At least he confines the statuary to the backyard."

She sighed. "But we have an entire garage full of statues of the saints: St. Francis of Assisi, St. Catherine, St. Augustine, St. John, even St. Ricky. Come out to the garage and I'll show you."

I followed her out and said, "St. Ricky?"

She showed me the statues in their garage. "He lived during the seventeenth century in Barbados. We'll have to put these statues out on the front lawn since the back is full. And I don't think the neighbors will be too pleased."

I said, "They probably won't mind, except perhaps the one of St. Ricky." I'm just not used to seeing a saint holding a bottle of tequila.

"The covenants in our neighborhood wouldn't permit it anyway. I know they don't say anything about prohibiting a statue of St. Ricky, but I'm sure the homeowners association will find a way to make us take it down. They're so rigid."

I said, "Some people are like that," thinking to myself that their neighbors don't know how lucky they are. I needed to check to make sure the covenants in my own neighborhood excluded ecclesiastical statuary.

I decided to try to console her. "With Dave it must be genetic. Remember that time his parents invited all of us over—and Dave's dad went on and on about the fireplace utensils he'd purchased even though he didn't have a fireplace?"

"You're right," Marlene said. "I hadn't thought of that before. Dave and his dad must share the same infomercial gene. I wonder if there's a cure for that."

I said doubtfully, "I think that researchers are focusing more on Alzheimer's, cancer, and heart disease. It's probably hard to get funding for research on the genetic propensity to buy useless items."

Marlene threw up her hands in the air. "That just goes to show you," she said indignantly.

I tried to nod sympathetically. I said, "I'm glad that Michael doesn't watch infomercials, because his dad bought all kinds of things they never used."

Later that evening, I walked in on Michael watching an infomercial. "Sweetheart," I shrieked, "turn that thing off! You don't want to get hooked!"

It was too late. He said, "But wait, there's more! I just ordered the Suck Up, which removes air from plastic bags and then seals them hermetically. We'll be able to keep lettuce fresh for eight and a half months."

I immediately got on the Internet. Somewhere, someone must be doing research on the infomercial gene.

I only hope they'll find a cure before a tequila-drinking saint shows up on our front lawn.

17

The Woman with the Perfect Driving Record

I was late for a meeting and got a speeding ticket. The policeman claimed I was going fifty-nine in a forty-five zone. Like that's even possible.

When I arrived at my women's group, I decided I would blame being late on the ticket.

"I'm sorry to be late. I got a ticket and, well, you know how long that takes." I tried to sound remorseful.

"Actually, Lauren, I don't," the chairwoman replied. "I've never received a speeding ticket."

A collective gasp arose from the room.

"Never?" I stared in disbelief. (Neither had my mother-in-law, but that was because she never drove over fifteen miles per hour.)

"Not even a parking fine," came the reply.

"Not even in high school?" someone asked.

"No." She was clearly enjoying this. It was probably a topic she introduced whenever possible.

My adolescence must have been a teensy bit spicier than

hers had been. I was from the old school of driving where you pull out of the parking lot and floor it.

The Woman with the Perfect Driving Record went on, "I simply have too much respect for the law to ever break the rules."

A wave of nausea spread throughout the room.

A discussion began over women who apply makeup while driving. Sinking down into my chair, I hoped no one had noticed the makeup mirror I had installed on my car visor.

"I hear they are going to start ticketing for that!" said one woman who was self-righteously wearing no makeup at all.

"Oh, great," I thought. I would have to remove those containers of cotton balls and moist towelettes I had superglued to my dashboard. And all my long-tube makeup and eyeliners had fit so nicely into those cup holders.

During the meeting, my mind drifted back to my very first ticket. I was sixteen years old, had my mom's car after school, and was cruising around with my friends. Apparently, I was driving a little too fast.

And of course I was looking particularly lovely in full battle-dress eyeliner and badly bleached hair. When the policeman asked for my license, I realize now that I probably shouldn't have asked him to hold the ice-cream cone I was eating.

As I thought back, I was amazed that I even passed the driver's test. I remembered that I was given the statement "If you are driving in a 30 mph zone and the person in front of you is going 25 mph, it's okay to speed up to 50 mph to pass him." I answered true. It is that kind of logic that makes sense to a sixteen-year-old, which is why none of us should ever leave our homes again.

At age seventeen, after I lamented to an older friend about the evils of getting a ticket simply for speeding, she gave me a tip. "Just bat your eyelashes and speak with an ever-so-slight Southern drawl."

For over twenty years, this worked well.

Then, when I was approaching forty (as if that weren't bad enough), I had my first encounter with a fifteen-year-old cop. He didn't seem to care about my eyelashes, my Southern accent, or anything else I tried to send his way.

That evening, I complained to Michael, "I am no longer little and cute to policemen."

"You were way overdue anyway," Michael replied unsympathetically. "You have just been skating by on those tickets for years."

Of course Michael thinks I'm a bad driver, but like I always say, why have a four-wheel-drive if you aren't going to drive over a few curbs?

18

The Woman Who Has Her Christmas Cards, Shopping, and Decorating Done Before Thanksgiving

Christmas is extremely stressful for me. Last year, on December 22, when I called my husband at work and his secretary said he was out of the office, a wild thought went through my head: "Gosh, what if Michael is having an affair? And if so, I wonder if the woman he's seeing would be willing to write the Christmas cards for his family this year so I don't have to do it."

When he came home later that day, I asked, "Are you having an affair?"

"Of course not."

"Are you sure?"

"Absolutely."

I shouted, "*Well, fine, I'll do* all *the Christmas cards again this year,*" and walked out of the room.

He followed me. "I believe the point here is that I'm not having an affair."

I said irritably, "Oh, sure, just see it from your perspective."

The next day, as I was composing our Christmas letter, I wrote that I had actually been so stressed out that I had hoped my husband had been having an affair so that this other woman could help me out with the Christmas cards. I decided to include a letter to the minister and his wife at the local church my husband and I attend, since I knew they had a sense of humor.

Shortly after Christmas, I volunteered with ten other women for an evening project at the church. We were hard at work when the minister's wife walked in. She exclaimed, "Lauren, I just loved your Christmas letter!"

"Oh, thanks."

Then she said, "And that part about your husband having the affair—I just loved it!"

Silence enveloped the room. Everyone's eyes focused on me. Without the use of clairvoyant abilities, I was able to determine that they were thinking:

1. "Why would anyone write about her husband having an affair in her Christmas letter?"
2. "Why would the minister's wife enjoy that so much?"

I cleared my throat. I looked around and mumbled, "Well, you know, you really had to read the whole letter." It was difficult to explain.

People find many different ways to be annoying before the holidays. A week prior to Thanksgiving a friend of mine called and said, "I'm having a party three days before Christmas."

"What? I'm at the peak of my shopping three days before Christmas."

"It's a potluck, so you need to bring a covered dish that'll serve forty people."

"Are you kidding? I barely have time to feed the cat before Christmas."

"And, by the way, we're doing a little gift exchange. Bring a wrapped gift suitable for a man or woman you don't know and keep the cost under two dollars. We'll open the gifts one by one to see who came up with the best one."

I shouted, *"I'm not coming to your stressful, time-consuming little party!"* and slammed down the receiver.

This led me to come up with the solution for the holidays: polygamy. While polygamy has been frowned upon in many circles, it deserves another look. It wouldn't have to be all year round—just a temporary "polygamy for the holidays" kind of arrangement. Think about it: you have one man and, say, six women. One woman does the holiday baking, one does the holiday decorating, one writes the cards, one buys the gifts, one wraps the gifts, and one pretends to enjoy herself. What could be better than this little plan? Are the wives of polygamists well rested during the holidays? Yes. Are they stressed out? No.

Every year on December 26, after I recover from all the tranquilizers I've taken, I think, "I've once again missed the meaning of Christmas." Which is why, next year during the summer months at the neighborhood pool, I'm going to start lining up dates for my husband.

19

The Husband Who Either Asks for Inane Instructions or Else Gives Inane Instructions

The other night before dinner, the following conversation occurred:

I said, "Michael, would you slice those potatoes for me?"

"Sure." Silence. "What do you want me to do with the potatoes again?"

"Cut them up."

"How do you want them cut?"

"Thin."

"Thin meaning paper-thin so you can see through them? Or thin meaning opaque?"

"Opaque."

"Okay, but how opaque? One-eighth inch, one-quarter inch, something in between?"

"One-eighth inch is fine," I said, holding up my fingers to show him how far apart.

He sighed.

I said, "What's wrong?"

"I don't know what you want."

"Why?"

"You said one-eighth inch but you demonstrated more like one-quarter inch."

"Just cut them up."

He began cutting up the potatoes. Then he said, "How do you want them arranged in the casserole dish? Do you want them stacked one on top of the other in rows going up and down? Or do you want them to overlap?"

"I want them to overlap. Don't forget, you need to salt them as you put them in."

"What?"

"Just add some salt."

"Where do I find the salt?"

"Do you really live here?"

"I just don't know where the salt is."

"It's in the cupboard with the spices."

"And that would be where?"

"Are you sure you're not just a guest in this house?"

"I found it. Now how much salt?"

"About half a teaspoon."

"You want each individual slice of potato salted? Or should I just add some here and there?"

"Just add some here and there."

"But then what happens if some of the slices don't get any?"

"It'll be fine."

"I'm beginning to get worried about it. I don't think each individual slice will have enough salt."

"It'll be fine."

"Are you sure?"

76

"I don't think the potatoes are the only thing to be worried about."

"What's that supposed to mean?"

"I'll be right back. I need to go and take some kind of pain reliever."

20

The Culinary Mom Who Brings Crab Aspic with Red Pepper Coulis to Her Child's School for Snacktime

One day outside my daughter's classroom, I saw the Culinary Mom. It was our day to bring snacks, and she had brought crab aspic with red pepper coulis. Unfortunately, the children loved it—go figure. I had brought a large bag of Sam's Club potato chips.

Sad to say, one day I had to drop off some school information to the Culinary Mom. Before I had time to say that I was late for something, anything, she pulled me into her house.

"I just wanted to show you my new Mauviel," she said with a ring of superiority in her voice. "They just arrived by messenger."

"Great," I said. "What are they?"

Silence. Then, "You don't know what Mauviel is?"

"No."

"Mauviel is the best copper cookware money can buy."

"I never use pots and pans, I just microwave."

She gasped in horror. "Without pots and pans, how do you make *poussins*?"

"I beg your pardon?"

"*Poussins*. You know, game hens?"

I was confused. Then I brightened. "You mean the rotisserie chicken at the supermarket?"

She gasped in horror again. "You don't eat those, do you?"

"Only on special occasions."

"But those supermarket chickens have no aroma, no taste, no piquancy."

I was confused again, but decided to just get used to it.

She went on, "Certainly you must have a pan to make crisp-fried julienne of leeks?"

It was hard to know how to respond.

———

Bad as she is, the Culinary Mom is no match for the Culinary Dad. And it doesn't take much for a man to define himself as a Culinary Dad, either. If they mix three ingredients together they believe they'll be asked to cater the *Vanity Fair* party next year after the Academy Awards.

We witnessed the Culinary Dad in action at a recent dinner party. He'd made the standard canned green bean casserole, but had decided to add fresh, not canned, mushrooms. He must have brought up this wild leap he had made into creative endeavors during the dinner conversation maybe six or seven times.

His wife, a true Culinary Mom, had made chicken Kiev in the likeness of Lenin's face. But of course the Culinary Dad couldn't even mention it.

———

One evening as we were eating dinner my husband said, "Wow, I was so impressed with that dinner the other night—that chicken Kiev really did look like Lenin. Why don't you ever do stuff like that?"

I looked at our dinner. "But honey, I did. See how I cut your meat loaf into the shape of the state of Colorado?"

"Why, yes, I hadn't noticed. How very nice."

Thank goodness my husband isn't a Culinary Dad. Little did he know that *all* meat loaf is cut into rectangles resembling the state of Colorado.

21

The Husband Who Has a Cold but Believes It's Malaria

When I was first married, I would get worried when my husband would catch a cold or the flu, because, from the way he complained, I truly believed him when he said he thought he was going to die. When he would stare vacantly ahead, as if he had just been told of an impending nuclear attack, I would think, "This must not be just a cold, it must be malaria like he claimed." I would get scared and rush him to the doctor, only to have him sent home with nose spray. Luckily, he wasn't sick very often.

One Saturday, I had a doctor's appointment. While still in bed, Michael asked, "Does our doctor make house calls?"

"Why?"

"I need to be seen also. But I'm too weak to get out of bed."

"I didn't even know you were sick."

"I've had this terrible flu for weeks now."

"The flu? I didn't know that. You've been going to work every day."

"I've been trying to go on in spite of this horrible disease, which is wreaking havoc with my sense of well-being."

I rolled my eyes with a look toward the heavens at all the women I knew who had moved on to the Other Side. The heavens smiled back. But I did call the doctor's office to see if Michael could sneak in to see the doctor during my appointment. They said they had time.

Soon after we arrived, we were ushered into the doctor's office. The nurse took our temperature, blood pressure, throat cultures, etc. My husband took about five minutes explaining to her in detail all his symptoms, and wondered if he might have double pneumonia and would need to be hospitalized. She left the room.

Then the physician walked in, examined both of us, and said to me, "You have severe bronchitis and a horrible sinus infection. You're positive for strep throat and you've got an ear infection in both ears. I'm giving you two kinds of antibiotics, a decongestant, cough medicine, and a steroid for ten days."

Michael said, "What about me?"

The doctor glanced casually at him and said, "You've got a case of the sniffles." He wrote "sniffles" in the diagnosis part of the medical statement and gave it to Michael.

"Surely I must need some kind of medication," he said indignantly.

"You might try some herbal tea."

My husband glared at him.

But once in a while miracles happen. A few months ago we met another couple, Jeff and Karen, after work for a quick dinner. Jeff walked into the restaurant with his right shoulder seven inches higher than his left, with his right arm limp at his side. Michael and I exclaimed, "Oh, no, what happened to you?"

Karen replied a little tersely, "He just gave blood."

I said, "Did something go wrong?"

"No, nothing went wrong. This is just how he acts after he gives blood."

Jeff sneered at her, holding his arm. "The needle stick was horrendous. You have no idea the amount of pain I'm in right now."

She said snidely, "Apparently not."

We were ushered to our table. Jeff had difficulty sliding into the booth, but eventually made it. Karen rolled her eyes.

When we were all seated, Karen said, "I don't know why you men are such martyrs."

He weakly held up the menu with his left hand, as his right arm remained limp at his side. She looked at him and rolled her eyes again. After we ordered I said, "What a great thing to do—to give blood."

He said, "Studies show that giving blood four times a year dramatically decreases a man's risk of heart disease and cancer. So I'd like to say that I'm giving blood out of the goodness of my heart, but it's actually to lower my risk of these two diseases. Karen wants me to do it so I'll be around longer."

She muttered under her breath, "I'll be so thrilled to have that."

"What did you say, honey?" He turned to her.

"I said I'll be so thrilled to have some food. I'm starving."

He said, "I'm starving, too. In fact, I'm feeling faint."

"Didn't they give you anything to eat after giving blood?"

"Lemonade, Lorna Doone cookies, and a Snickers bar."

"Well, then, you should be fine."

He leaned forward and held his head in his hands. "Tell them to bring us some food, any food, right away. I think I'm going into shock."

She just stared at him and didn't move a muscle.

He looked at her out of the corner of his eye, straightened up, and said, "But I'm feeling better now."

She turned to me. "How's the writing going?"

I smiled. "I'm finding more material all the time."

Our food arrived. Jeff ate with his left hand, which was noticeably awkward, but Karen pretended not to notice. Then the check came. Jeff reached back with his left hand and struggled and struggled to remove his wallet from the back right pocket of his pants. He finally came up with it and placed it on the table.

And then the climactic moment occurred. While his right arm remained limp at his side, Jeff, with a great deal of effort, fished the money out of his wallet using only his left hand. It took several minutes to get the money out, as well as to put back in everything else that had fallen out of his wallet. We all sat looking at him and then we all looked at each other.

And that's when the best part of all happened. Jeff realized how he looked trying to remove money from his wallet with one hand and, miraculously, smiled to himself. And then the rest of us smiled. And then he began to laugh, and then we all laughed until we hurt.

I thought, "What a breakthrough for medical science."

22

The Mom Who Throws a Cinderella Birthday Party for Her Daughter by Installing a Drawbridge to the Front Door and Digging a Moat Around the House

My daughter's first two birthday parties were a snap. All adults, a few pink decorations, and Krispy Kreme doughnuts.

But by the time Caroline turned three, she had many friends of her own. I innocently invited twelve children to her party. My husband and I played "duck, duck, goose" with them, and "bounce the balloon in the air," and then we did a craft project I had planned where they glued elbow macaroni onto construction paper. Unfortunately, all of this took only fifteen minutes. You soon learn that when you have twelve kids in your home, time becomes warped and what seems like seven hours is only about six minutes.

We moved on to cake. I had purchased a cake at the grocery store, but had forgotten to buy candles. I searched the house completely and finally found three large pillar candles I had purchased about a month after Caroline was born. I had waited since then for the moment my husband

and I could use them for a romantic evening. The candles had never been lit, if you know what I mean.

So the cake had three candles, the kids all had fun, and later that evening after Caroline had fallen asleep, we called a visiting nurses temp agency to help us get up off the couch.

About six months later, I had the misfortune to run up against . . . the Perfect Birthday Mom. Her daughter sent out a birthday invitation to my daughter and before long the happy day arrived. As we walked up the sidewalk, we saw that a water-filled moat had been dug out around the house, and a drawbridge was being let up and down at the front door into what had become "Cinderella's Castle." I was stunned.

For the first activity, the Perfect Birthday Mom had made a huge piñata in the likeness of Cinderella's evil stepmother. The girls took turns trying to knock it silly. When it opened, beautiful little treasures fell out, such as hand-embroidered doll dresses in the Cinderella birthday theme. I was overwhelmed.

Then the Perfect Birthday Mom announced it was craft time. This involved putting together an intricate design of jewels that each girl could attach to a Tiffany-quality lampshade for her own room. I felt weak all over.

But the party favors were the final, spectacular finish to this birthday celebration. Each girl was given a huge, beautifully wrapped box containing a Cinderella dress hand-sewn by the Perfect Birthday Mom. Each girl's dress fit perfectly.

I ran to my car and downed some Prozac that I keep locked in the glove compartment for emergencies.

After the party, I displayed symptoms of post-traumatic stress disorder. I had nightmares that I had fallen into the moat while leading my daughter across the drawbridge only to be attacked by an alligator that had the face of the Perfect Birthday Mom. Or I would dream that at my daughter's next birthday party, our party favor to our guests consisted of week-old Krispy Kreme doughnuts.

A few weeks before Caroline's fourth birthday, I said to Michael, "Okay, for Caroline's next birthday, we need to do better. We can't expect to keep sliding through these parties with nothing but some Elmer's glue and macaroni. We need to keep up. Do you have any suggestions?"

He thought for a full minute and then said, "No."

"Why don't we hire someone to do her party this year?"

"Really," he said excitedly, "you can find people out there who are willing to entertain twelve four-year-olds for three hours?"

"It might be a little expensive."

"Of course it would be expensive. It's asking a great deal of someone in terms of emotional, physical, and mental stamina. Even if it requires refinancing our house, let's do it."

So we hired Silly the Clown. She was worth every penny of her craft-worthy soul. My husband and I vacillated between the video camera and our afternoon tea. Silly was a little slice of heaven sent down just for those of us who can't tell the difference between papier-mâché and a paper shredder (I always get those two mixed up).

After that party I was able to reduce the amount of my antidepressants again. My nightmares stopped. We had Silly back for the fifth birthday, and then the sixth. Sure, our mortgage payments have increased. But life is good again.

23

The Craft Mom Who Sends You an Exquisitely Handmade Thank-You Note for the Baby Gift You Sent to Her Fourth Child

If you have a child, especially a daughter, sooner or later you'll encounter the Craft Mom. She loves coming up with new and exciting craft projects for her daughter to do with friends. Before you know it, you'll feel completely inadequate. Why? Let me count the ways.

The first time Caroline visited her new friend's house, she returned home having made an exquisitely designed, hand-crafted, beaded purse, similar to the ones they sell in Neiman Marcus for four hundred dollars.

The second time Caroline visited the Craft Mom's home, she returned with a sixteen-by-twenty picture of herself and her new friend. It had a handcrafted frame that the Craft Mom helped my daughter carefully prime and cover with a metallic coating, making it suitable for hanging in the Metropolitan Museum of Art.

The third time will be the final one for reasons that will soon be all too obvious. After this latest encounter with the Craft Mom, my child returned home having made a two-foot-by-five-foot stained-glass picture depicting the Last Supper. This masterpiece stands on a harp-like pedestal, which the Craft Mom carefully unloaded in my driveway from the back of her Suburban.

Even after having her fourth child, the Craft Mom sent me a handmade thank-you note for the baby shower I attended. The note is written on paper that she made herself, and even includes heartfelt thanks for running out to her car and getting the diaper bag during the baby shower. In contrast, after Caroline was born, I simply took ads out in newspapers in all the major cities that had people sending us gifts. If they couldn't be bothered to notice the half-inch ad in the personals section, it wasn't my fault.

Finally, I couldn't avoid it any longer. I invited Caroline's new friend over. After she arrived, the conversation went something like this:

Caroline said, "So, Mom, since Melissa and I made such neat things at her house, what can we make here?"

"Uh . . . well . . . umm . . . gee . . . I suppose we could try to find some glue somewhere and glue something together."

They looked at each other.

My daughter said, "I think you used up all the glue when you tried to glue that picture to the wall because you couldn't find any picture hooks."

"Oh, that's right. Maybe we could cut something up instead. I have some paper in the computer printer. No, check that. I forgot that we're out. But there must be paper in this house somewhere."

They watched as I searched the house for paper and finally found some in the fax machine. I said, "Now, for the scissors. I think I saw some in the garage a few weeks ago."

They looked at each other again.

"Ah, Mom, I think that we'll just skip the craft project today?

"I wouldn't hear of it. Take out some canned vegetables and we can trace around the bottom of the cans, and then cut out some lovely circles. Doesn't that sound nice?"

They both looked at their feet.

"Mom, you know, maybe we'll just watch a video."

"I've got it! Let's string some Cheerios and make garlands for the birds—except I'm out of Cheerios so we'd have to use Rice Krispies. And I don't have string but we could use dental floss."

"That's okay, Mom."

"We could go out and look for some rocks and then dip them in food coloring. Except the only food coloring I have left is brown. So I guess they'd just end up looking like rocks."

"Really, Mom, I don't think . . ."

"We could take some egg cartons and make lovely jewelry boxes out of them."

My daughter said quickly, "Mom, I just remembered I was going to clean my room."

Her friend nodded. "I'd be happy to help her."

"Whatever you think, but I'm happy to do a project with you two. Maybe we could see if we still have some Play-Doh in the house."

They gasped and ran out of the room, grateful to escape into housework.

24

The Perfect Grocery Store Mom Who Always Goes Through the Check-Out Lane Quickly

Just yesterday, I had a close encounter with the Perfect Grocery Store Mom.

After frantically driving up and down all the parking aisles in the supermarket parking lot, I finally found a spot at the farthest end of the main aisle. I then made the half-mile trek to the store.

During my hike I noticed a car pulling into the spot closest to the entrance. Out came the Perfect Grocery Store Mom. She was wearing a warm-up suit trimmed with gold edging. She wore beautiful gold jewelry to match. Even her tennis shoes had gold laces. Accompanying her was her beautifully dressed child. They both appeared *happy* to be grocery shopping.

We entered the store at the same time. Usually I hung around the baked goods section for the free samples, but I decided to try and keep up with the Perfect Grocery Store Mom instead.

I followed her into the produce section and noticed that

she masterfully ripped open a plastic produce bag and placed asparagus in it all with one hand, while continuing to drive the cart with the other.

I also noticed her stash of coupons. I overheard her daughter asking her why she used coupons. "Darling," said the Perfect Grocery Store Mom, "last year I saved enough on groceries for all of us to take that trip around the world. Remember?"

"Oh, yes, Mommy, that was wonderful."

I felt sick.

She moved on to canned goods while I stopped to ask a woman who worked in the bakery department if she could decipher my grocery list for me. She called a few guys in the meat department over to help and we all finally figured out that the item I had written down that looked like "chilled lava" was actually "distilled water."

By now, the Perfect Grocery Store Mom had gained considerably on me. And then I fell even farther behind because my shopping cart lost one of its wheels. I flagged down an employee to show him. He just handed me a screwdriver and kept walking.

I finally got tired of reattaching the wheel and decided to just check out and call my husband to pick up the other things I needed on his way home from work.

The Perfect Grocery Store Mom pulled into the checkout area just as I did. The manager noticed her pull up and ran over to open a lane for her. I went over to another lane. Just then bulbs began to flash and confetti was streaming everywhere. Over the loudspeaker I heard, "And now, on aisle six we have our fifty thousandth customer. And in celebration of this event, she has won free groceries for a year!" Balloons floated down from the ceiling, and the winner was: the Perfect Grocery Store Mom.

As I approached my checkout clerk, she said to me, "They want a group shot of all of us clerks with the fifty thousandth customer, so I'll be right back." I busied myself with the current magazines.

I read an article on how Camilla Parker Bowles loves to go bowling, just as her last name sort of implies, and I read that cracking your knuckles is the result of a release of gas in the joint fluid—who knew? Finally, my clerk returned.

"Wasn't that something?" she said joyously. "What luck, to be the fifty thousandth customer."

"Yeah, right," I said.

She began checking out my groceries. "Oh, sorry," she said. "I have to leave again. My register tape just ran out and I'll need to go to the back storeroom to get some more."

I sighed. "Can't I just move to another checkout lane?"

"That'll screw up our entire system, since I've already started checking out your groceries. I'll be right back."

While I was waiting, one of the managers went by with the two-hundred-dollar floral arrangement for the Perfect Grocery Store Mom. As he passed me the CONGRATULATIONS sign on top of the flowers fell over and broke eight of my dozen eggs.

I continued to busy myself with magazines. I read about how to decorate your living room using nothing but birdhouses, how to disguise a carrot soufflé so your children and husband will eat it (you completely cover it with butter brickle candy), and the most surprising article of all: "How to Achieve Emotional Balance by Raising Bees."

By then the festivities had made their way outside, so at least I didn't have to listen to the Perfect Grocery Store Mom's acceptance speech over the loudspeaker anymore. I asked another clerk in the lane next to me when she thought my clerk might return with the tape.

She said, "I got the last roll of tape in the back storeroom this morning. But a truck's supposed to come in with more tape."

I looked around and assessed the situation. I had eight cracked eggs, I had read all of the magazines, and my only hope of a clerk rested on a truck that's "supposed to come in with more tape."

I decided to just give up, leave the store, and ask my husband to pick up everything. I made the long trek to my car, got in, and began driving. Just as I was about to drive by the Perfect Grocery Store Mom's car, she backed out and blocked the aisle. Then a crew of reporters from Channel 11 pulled up in front of her and ran up and asked if they could get some footage. They hollered at me that it would only take about half an hour. I turned and looked back to see if I could back up, but noticed crews from Channels 3, 5, 8, and 10 pulling up behind me.

Suddenly I snapped. I just couldn't take it anymore. I slumped over the steering wheel of my car, sobbing uncontrollably. Just then my cell phone rang. It was Michael.

"Honey, are you in your car crying?"

"Yes," I said, surprised. "How did you know?"

He said, "Well, you're on TV—you're on Channel 11, in fact, I am flipping through the channels and all the major networks have you on. You're even on CNN."

I looked around, stunned. I slunk down in the car seat.

Michael continued, "Just lie low for a few minutes. I'll tell you when the cameras move off you and then you can get out. I'll come and get you."

"Fine," I said hysterically. "I'll meet you inside the store," I said in between sobs.

After I made it into the store, I headed straight for the bakery section. I found that I still had the strength to select a couple of cake doughnuts with chocolate frosting. They were delicious. I felt considerably better. Then I tried some lemon pastries, which were tart without being overpowering. Life was looking up. And then I had to try the little raspberry-filled cookies, which were flaky and juicy. I sighed, contentedly.

Considering everything that had happened, my trip to the grocery store really turned out pretty well.

25

The Wife Who Finds Something Wrong with the Way Her Husband Saved the Life of the Man Choking at the Table Next to Them

We went out to dinner the other night with the "it's never quite good enough" wife. She complained about everything and anything, including all of her husband's past sins. Even after he had nearly performed a miracle at one point during the dinner by resuscitating the gentleman at the table next to us, she could still find something wrong: "Good grief, Kevin, couldn't you have managed to do the Heimlich without spilling the squash soup all over the table?"

While attending a wedding the next afternoon, my mind wandered and I began to think how differently history would have been written if Jesus had decided to get married to the "it's never quite good enough" wife. It may have gone something like this:

Jesus returns home after a particularly draining day. His wife, Stella, says:

"Good Lord! Where in God's name have you been? You smell awful!"

"Well, as a matter of fact, I just raised Lazarus from the dead. It took a lot out of me."

"Well, I should think so, especially the spring morning freshness I had worked so hard to get into your clothes. Before you did that, did you consider all the work it would create for me? It'll take me a month to get that robe smelling decent again. Why did you have to wait until he smelled like a farm animal to raise him from the dead?"

"Because people were amazed since he had been dead for four days."

"Well, if you really wanted to amaze people, why not bring back Socrates or Plato? Those are people who have been dead for four hundred years."

"Well, I never thought of that."

"Four days is nothing. This is just like that little fiasco the other night when you turned the water into wine at the Shapiro girl's wedding."

"But they couldn't believe it—the bride's mother fainted with astonishment."

"And do you know why that was?"

"I thought it was because she had never seen anyone turn water into wine before."

"No, it was because they were serving poultry, and you came up with a merlot. Everyone *knows* you don't drink red wine with chicken."

"Oh." He looks a little dejected. "Well, I thought it was good."

"Quite frankly, sweetheart, the wine was a little dry."

"Oh." He looks even more dejected.

"Well, I'm sure you'll do better next time. Maybe something more fruity, more aromatic."

"Well, I'll try," he says, looking preoccupied.

"And while we're on the subject, you know the other day when you had Peter throw out the nets to catch the fish? What did you bring up from the bottom of the Sea of Galilee? Haddock. I couldn't believe it. Who eats haddock? Maybe next time you could try for some nice trout. I mean, if you're going to expend all this energy on these 'miracles' as you call them, maybe you could go the extra mile and come up with something really good."

"Well, I guess you're right."

"It's also like the episode with the multitudes when you came up with the loaves and fishes. Did you ever consider that maybe those people would need a filet knife, a frying pan, olive oil, plates, a tablecloth, napkins to match, and salt and pepper? And then you completely forgot about any kind of beverage."

"Oh, yeah, I guess I did."

"Well, I'm sure you'll get it right eventually. You just need to give it some time. And frankly, there isn't a lot of money in turning water into wine or bringing up tons of fish unless you come up with some kind of a marketing plan. And again, as I see it, it's the quality that would hurt us. There isn't a lot of demand these days for cheap red wine and haddock."

"No, I suppose not. In fact, now that you mention it, maybe I'll go back into some of that carpentry work I used to do."

"That's a good idea. It's best not to get into all these other ventures that will never go anywhere."

26

The Woman Who Has Dinner Completed Every Day by Ten a.m.

For my daughter's school picnic, we were supposed to deliver our food to the chairman's house the day prior to the festivities. It was then that I encountered the Woman Who Has Dinner Completed Every Day by Ten a.m.

"Why didn't you just put those beans into a Crock-Pot?" the chairman quizzed as she led me into her newly remodeled kitchen.

"I'm sorry," I apologized automatically. "It didn't say anything about Crock-Pots in the picnic flyer."

"That really goes without saying, doesn't it?" she smiled benevolently. "I mean, this is the twenty-first century."

I thought Crock-Pots had gone out with big hair, but I said nothing.

She added helpfully, "You can do anything in slow cookers with today's advanced technology."

We then went into her kitchen. With a dramatic sweep of her arms, she opened floor-to-ceiling folding doors to reveal one entire wall-sized grid of shelves containing Crock-Pots.

There were six Crock-Pots across and five Crock-Pots down. It was staggering.

"Last year I did my entire Thanksgiving dinner in Crock-Pots," she gushed. "This giant green one is my special turkey roaster. It takes about six days for a twenty-five pound turkey."

"Oh, please," I thought to myself. She noticed that I was looking at how each Crock-Pot was plugged into its own outlet.

"I had to have industrial-strength 440-voltage wiring installed," she explained. "The contractor was hesitant since they only use this kind of wiring in factories where they make heavy machinery, but it was a small price to pay for real power." I began to feel a little apprehensive.

She continued, "Last summer I had the kitchen stove removed because I never used it." I didn't use my stove either, but I still thought it looked appropriate in the kitchen.

Though the wall of Crock-Pots appeared ominous to me, I had to admit that some of the pots were emitting wonderful aromas. I had reached for the lid of a pot in the dessert row when the Woman Who Has Dinner Completed Every Day by Ten a.m. shrieked, "Don't lift that lid! You'll let all the steam out! There's a chocolate soufflé in there."

"Sorry," I murmured. I was obviously way out of my depth here.

She talked on. "This light blue pot is very special. It keeps Krispy Kreme doughnuts at the perfect temperature for optimal texture."

Suddenly, she had my full attention. "You're really devoted to this whole concept, aren't you?"

She blushed slightly at this. "Well," she demurred, "I am

the secretary-treasurer of the International Slow-Cookers Society. I love the group, but it's becoming too political."

"Political?"

"A group of troublemakers has formed over 'high' versus 'low' settings. To make matters worse, a small group has started a big fuss over dairy. I don't know how much more we can take."

I nodded, not really listening, because I began to think about something very important. She continued on and on, until I finally had to cut in.

"I'm sorry," I said apologetically, "but I have to know something immediately. How much would one of those light blue crockpots cost; you know, the ones that keep the Krispy Kreme doughnuts warm?"

She smiled. "$199.95. And you also might need to rewire your kitchen."

I smiled back with a sigh of relief. It would be worth every penny.

27

The Husband Who Spends Thirty Minutes Taking a Picture of Jasmine at Disney World

We first had the pleasure of meeting Jasmine at Disneyland, and she quickly became Caroline's favorite princess.

Apparently, however, the Jasmine in California is not *exactly* like the Jasmine we met in Florida during our trip to Disney World. The Jasmine at Disney World was even more spectacular, if you know what I mean. It must be that since there is so much water in Florida, the survival of the fittest dictates that only the Jasmines with the greatest upper-body buoyancy will survive.

As we stood in line waiting to see Jasmine, we caught glimpses here and there but didn't get to see her up close until we arrived at the front of the line. When we got there, Caroline had Jasmine sign her autograph book and then quickly assumed her place beside Jasmine for the photo.

They posed nicely for the picture. Jasmine leaned forward, giving even greater exposure. But Michael, who had the camera, didn't move. He stood perfectly motionless, staring at

Jasmine. He then sighed contentedly as if he had just achieved inner peace.

I said, "Aren't you going to take the picture?"

"What picture?" he said softly, keeping his eyes on Jasmine.

"The one of Caroline and Jasmine."

"A picture of Jasmine?" he said, turning to me wide-eyed.

"Well, of course," I said impatiently.

"Oh, for God's sakes, I'll do that right now," he said, running up close to get the shot.

I could tell he had the camera aimed a little high, so I yelled, "Try to get all of Caroline in the picture."

"Who?"

"Caroline."

"I don't know who you mean."

"*Caroline, your daughter.*"

"Oh, yeah, right."

We all stood there waiting. Finally I said, "What is taking you so long?"

He kept staring into the camera.

I said, "Michael, are you going to take the picture?"

He kept staring into the camera.

"*Michael!*" I yelled.

He finally turned to me. "Did you ask me a question?"

"Yes."

"What was it?"

"Are you going to take a picture of Caroline and Jasmine?"

"A picture of Jasmine," he said softly, with a faraway look in his eyes.

"Oh, for heaven's sake," I said.

104

An attendant who was monitoring the line said to me, "Don't worry, this happens all the time. At least your husband doesn't mind having your daughter in the picture. A lot of times they only want Jasmine."

She continued. "In fact, we have a lot of dads who come through the line all by themselves. They leave their wife and kids in Frontierland and then run full out over here to Adventureland for another look at Jasmine. In fact," she said, motioning to a guy sprinting up to the end of the line, "here comes one now."

The man rushed up to the end of the line and then leaned over, clutching his knees and gasping for air.

"See what I mean?" she said to me.

I rolled my eyes and turned back to Michael. "Will you just take the picture?"

"Just one more minute," he said impatiently.

Finally, we all heard the click.

"Thank goodness," I said. "Now can we get out of here? If we hurry, we can make it to the Pirates of the Caribbean before our FASTPASS expires."

"You want to leave Jasmine?" he asked, astonished.

Caroline and I began walking away. After we'd gone about fifty feet, I noticed that Michael wasn't with us.

I looked back and saw him leaning against a wall. His face was glowing as if he had just returned from Mount Tabor after witnessing the transfiguration of Jesus.

Caroline ran back. *"Dad!"* she hollered. *"We're going now."* She grabbed his hand and pulled him away.

When they caught up to me, I said to him, "Do you need some oxygen?"

He looked relieved. "Do they have oxygen around here?" he asked, sitting down on a bench and wiping the sweat off his forehead.

"Oh, please," I said sarcastically, but thinking to myself that it wouldn't be such a bad idea.

After we arrived at the Pirates of the Caribbean and had been standing in line for a few minutes, Michael said, "You know, I've been thinking that we need a meeting place in case we get separated from one another. In case all of a sudden, you two look around and I'm not there. And I was just thinking, how about if we designate Jasmine as our meeting place?"

Well, as they say, the Magic Kingdom has something for everyone.

28

The Woman Who Receives Martha Stewart's E-Mail "Thought for the Day" and Is Too Scared to Delete It

My friend Michelle caught up with me while I was picking up Caroline from school one day. She said, "You look exhausted. Are you okay?"

"Oh, I've had such a busy week."

"What's been going on?"

"Well, I've been receiving Martha Stewart's 'Thought for the Day' on my e-mail and I'm having a hard time keeping up."

"Why?"

"Because on Monday the thought for the day was to spray your shoe racks with a jasmine-clover-scented oil. I had to go to five places before I finally found oil with the correct percentages of jasmine and clover. That took up Monday and some of Tuesday. Then on Tuesday the thought for the day was to rip out the tiles in your bathroom and replace them with painted cracked-eggshell tiles that you make yourself. By the time I returned the jackhammer I had rented from Home Depot, it was almost ten p.m. on Thursday. So then

I got behind on the Wednesday and Thursday thoughts for the day and started those on Friday. But it has just escalated. I'm so behind now that I'll be doing the fall projects she suggests sometime in early March."

My friend looked perplexed. "Why can't you just ignore the thought for the day, or delete them?"

I said quietly, "I don't think Martha would like that."

"Oh, for heaven's sakes. Just click 'unsubscribe' on the bottom of the e-mail."

Again I said quietly, "I actually looked for that link, but there isn't one. Like I said, I don't think Martha would like it."

"Oh, you're hopeless," she said as she walked away.

She obviously didn't realize who I was up against. For many years now Martha has been determined to raise the standards of America's homes, and has been pretty persistent about achieving that goal. And who knows what she picked up in prison. Frankly, I was scared to death of what would happen if I did delete one of her thoughts for the day, let alone try to unsubscribe.

Weeks went by where I was unable to even eat during the day because I was so busy cleaning out my rain gutters with a Clorox solution followed by a spritz of lemon. I exhausted myself from making Polish pastries with names I couldn't pronounce. Squaring off the bedsheets took most of one afternoon (and irritated the cat, who was trying to sleep).

But then a little piece of luck came my way: a virus invaded my PC and wiped out my entire computer. I happily reunited with my family that evening. I was surprised at how much Caroline had grown. Michael looked as if he had gained weight, probably since he hadn't been eating my cooking. And then, even though it was the middle of April, we all exchanged Christmas gifts. They gave me scented oil, but unfortunately, it did not have the correct percentages of jasmine and clover.

Later that evening after they had gone to bed, I poured the oil down the drain. I just couldn't risk having Martha find out.

29

The Babysitter Who Is Better at Everything Than You Are

I used to be a fairly popular person. But the day I went back to work and Jill came to live with us, that all began to change.

The first time I noticed this was when I received a baby shower invitation for a neighbor with Jill's name prominently placed on the front of the card, and my name scribbled on the back as an afterthought. I thought it was odd.

The next week I took a few hours off work and walked into Caroline's third-grade class to volunteer. As I came in the door, all the children in the class and the teacher looked up expectantly and then I watched their faces fall as they saw it was me, and not Jill. One little snot-nosed kid said sweetly, "Mrs. Perry, when will Jill come back to see us?" "Oh, fine," I thought. "I could be out enjoying lunch with a friend, but no, I'm here to report on Jill's whereabouts." Ignoring his question, I pointed out all the spelling errors in his report on Eleanor Roosevelt, which made me feel better about myself because I am an excellent speller and he isn't.

At Caroline's ninth birthday party, when Jill taught the girls to knit a striped pair of gloves with fingers alternating in fuchsia and purple, I asked one of the moms if she had read any good books. "Oh, I forgot you were here!" she replied. "I was just listening to Jill discuss French literature with the girls."

Another mom walked up. "I didn't know Louis XIV used to give speeches on horticulture," she said in a shocked voice. "And I graduated from Oxford. Jill really knows her French history."

Another mom chimed in. "Well, the other afternoon during the break at soccer practice, Jill went out and fixed the transmission on my car. We've had that car in to seven different mechanics, and none of them have been able to do what Jill did."

Another mom said, "Jill gave me a great stock tip and now I'm fifteen thousand dollars richer than I was last week at this time."

Finally, one of the moms noticed that I was feeling left out. She said, "Lauren, share with everyone your exciting news from last week."

"Oh," I said modestly, "it was nothing."

"No, really, tell everyone."

"Okay," I said. "Did any of you know that I was able to eat dinner one evening last week without spilling on myself?"

They all looked at each other.

Another mom broke into the conversation. "Jill showed me how to fix my own computer. And," she said importantly, "Jill is having lunch with me next week."

Everyone's eyes grew large.

"She is?" asked one of the moms. "How did you manage that?"

"Well, during the reception after Jill unveiled her latest sculpture in the Castle Rock Town Square, I asked her if maybe we could have lunch, and she said 'Sure.'"

"Wow," one of the other moms whispered. "Lunch with Jill!"

One by one the other moms quickly began asking, "Can I come, too?" "Can I?" "Please, can I?"

"No," said the favored one. "It's just going to be Jill and me. And that's it. I asked first."

The group looked crestfallen.

The preferentially treated mom whispered in a conspiratorial tone, "She's going to give me the formula she uses for cleaning the garage floor."

The group was aghast.

Another mom said wistfully, "I hear that when she's done cleaning the garage floor, she follows with Pledge floor wax."

The group murmured its admiration.

I decided to change the subject. "Time for Caroline to open presents."

Another mom said, "Lauren, do you mind if I have the leftover paper? Jill showed me how to wallpaper a bedroom using nothing but used wrapping paper."

"Fine," I shouted. *"Take it."*

No one noticed my irritation.

"Mrs. Perry," said one of Caroline's guests, "can I have another piece of the cake that Jill made from scratch? It was wonderful."

I slapped a piece of cake on her plate. A mom said, "Isn't that cake the incredible Sacher torte, from the famous Hotel Sacher in Vienna?"

Jill nodded.

I looked around. Then I cleared my throat and announced, "I made a tater-tot hotdish last week."

No one said anything. Everyone was crowding around Jill, asking her for the torte recipe.

Oh, well. At least I can spell better than some third grader.

30

The Husband Who Doesn't Notice When His Wife Redecorates the Living and Dining Rooms

After our annual Christmas party last year, I told Michael we needed to redecorate our living and dining rooms.

"I'm tired of this boring beige," I complained in my whiniest, most irritating voice. Michael, very familiar with this voice, usually capitulates immediately when he hears it. That's why I was surprised when he balked.

"Are you crazy? This place looks great the way it is. You can do whatever you want, but don't involve me." I took this as a green light.

The next day, I swung into action. I asked an interior designer friend to help me make a list of what to do.

"I have a great team of handymen," she said enthusiastically. "They are very reasonable and will do anything if you provide them with pizzas. Let's start with new carpeting in January and see if your husband notices."

It was a plan. Michael departed for his office, and the carpet truck arrived two minutes later. The new carpeting looked beautiful and I was ecstatic!

Caroline gasped when she came home from school. I explained that she shouldn't exactly lie to Daddy outright if he asked her if this was new carpeting, but told her not to volunteer any information. I thought this would be good training for her own future relationships.

Michael arrived home, never even glancing into the living room, and asked, "Do I smell pizza?"

"We had some for lunch," I murmured, kissing him on the cheek.

In February, I had the couch reupholstered. It was gone for a week, but Michael didn't go into the living room.

In March, I had wanted to paint the walls, but the designer thought Michael might notice the smell, so we sneaked in a new fireplace screen. No comments from Michael.

In April, I found a great deal on a giant mirror for the dining room. It was beautiful.

May was warm enough to open all the windows, so while Michael took Caroline and her friends to the community swimming pool, I painted the walls. They looked great.

In June, I talked Michael into a romantic weekend in Vail. Caroline's babysitter supervised the crown molding installation in the dining room. It was perfect.

July brought a new dining table. I decided to go with a round, glass-topped table to replace the wooden, rectangular one. We had dinner on it the next night, but I just used candles, so no one noticed.

I was really enjoying this.

Over the next few months, new chairs, curtains, and lamps were changed out for the old ones.

While we went out of state for Michael's high school reunion in October, a gorgeous new chandelier was installed in the dining room. I felt my renovation was complete.

In mid-November, a flyer came from our TV cable company offering more sports channels. I thought it would be a nice surprise for Michael. The cable company installed the new channels, and when Michael arrived home from work, we had a football game on.

"Something is different here! I can just feel it," he said.

"Oh, Daddy! You're right!" Caroline gushed. "It's a surprise! We ordered some new sports channels for you!"

Amazing. She would have cracked like an egg the minute he asked her about new carpeting. Purely on the basis of genetics, I would have expected better from her. Oh, well, she was still young.

Flipping through all the new channels, Michael was a happy guy for the next three days. I made a mental note that the next redecorating we'll do will be to build a soundproof booth for him to watch TV without me.

When the night of the annual party arrived, I was ready. All the women oohed and aahed over the changes. None of the men noticed anything except the new channels. We all had a great evening.

While we were cleaning up after everyone had left, Michael talked about the evening. "I received loads of compliments on all your new decorating. The house looks beautiful, and I appreciate all the hard work you and your designer put in on it."

I stared at him in disbelief. "I thought you didn't notice a thing. How long have you known?"

"Well," he replied, "I saw your list shortly after we talked about redecorating, about a year ago. And, well, I waved to the carpet guys when I left for work that day. But you get so much more done when you think you are sneaking around that I thought it would be best if I played along. I *do* think you paid too much for that dining room mirror, though." He laughed as he wandered off to bed.

I just smiled. After all, a man's house is his castle.

31

The Perfect Feng Shui Woman Who Has a Bagua Map and Knows How to Use It

The other day I had to run by another mom's home to drop off material for the next PTA meeting. As I walked up to the front door, I noticed a beautiful hyacinth wreath hanging on the door with exquisite topiary on either side. When she answered the door, I handed over the materials to her, but before I left, I commented on the entrance to her home.

"Oh, Lauren," she enthused, "everyone knows that a hyacinth wreath placed at your front door will bring vital energy into your home. You know, it's feng shui, the study of how to arrange your environment to enhance your life. You use a bagua map to chart where each of the major areas of your life is represented in your home. Come on in and I'll show you."

Following her in, I immediately felt a sense of peace and tranquility. I could hear the sound of water running over rocks. She said, "Every piece of furniture and every object has been strategically placed in a way which gives rise to the steady movement of chi, or energy, through the house."

I was impressed.

She continued, "Since I had my house redone by a feng shui consultant, you wouldn't believe the changes in our lives. My mother, who lives with us, had a deadly disease but after she hung a crystal at her bedroom window, she was cured. After we placed purple curtains in my son's room, he made the varsity football team as a freshman in high school, and he'd never even *played* football before. And we moved the position of the bed in the master bedroom; after that, my husband was awarded the Nobel Peace Prize."

Now I was really impressed. I asked, "What is a bagua map?"

"Oh," she said, "it's how you map out various rooms in your house according to important aspects of life, including health, wealth, and happiness. The bagua map charts the energy each of these aspects of life gathers in your home."

I decided that I had to get my hands on her feng shui consultant. I asked for her number.

"Oh," she said, "she's on a trip around the world. But you could hire someone else or do it yourself."

I thought to myself, "Well, how hard can it be? I'll just save some money on a consultant and instead buy a book and feng shui my own way to health and happiness."

Since Michael was going to be away on a business trip for a few days, I thought it would be the perfect time to implement a few changes around the house.

I started the second day he was gone, and got everything done that morning. I was pleased with the results. Later that afternoon my neighbor, who works as a nurse, stopped by.

She said, "Lauren, I see you have placed tiny mirrors around some of your trees in the front yard. What are you doing?"

"Well," I said smugly. "Everyone knows that you need to enhance the important people and travel aspects of your bagua map, and there's no better way to do it than to place mirrors around your fruit trees at ninety-degree angles."

She replied, "I have no idea what you're talking about."

I spoke as an authority. "You know, feng shui. Come on in, I'll show you how I've enhanced the chi energy in my house. I did it while Michael was out of town—he should be back soon."

When we walked into the house, the front door banged as it failed to open all the way. My neighbor said, "That's odd. Your front door won't open all the way."

"Well," I said with a ring of superiority, "that's because I moved the bed from the master bedroom down here to the front hall."

She said, "I don't understand what you're saying now, either."

I turned sideways to get in through the front door. She followed.

"See," I said proudly. "I moved our bed down from the master bedroom into the front hall of the house. Now the chi energy can't escape through the front door. Besides, I needed the space in the master bedroom since that is the wealth and prosperity area on our bagua map. I needed to remove the bed to make way for something that really needed to be there."

She said, "What could be more important in a bedroom than a bed?"

I said defensively, "A giant rock."

"You put a giant rock in your bedroom instead of a bed?"

"Yes, and I painted it red, to attract greater wealth into our lives."

She said, "Are you dizzy or feeling faint? Can you lift up your arms and stick out your tongue at the same time? Try and smile for me, would you?"

I knew she was checking to make sure I hadn't had a stroke.

I said irritably, "I'm fine. It's just that I'm into feng shui right now. This stuff really works."

"No, really. When was your last checkup? Have you had your blood pressure taken recently? No, wait. I'll just go home and get my cuff."

She left in a hurry.

Just then I heard the garage door go up. In a few moments, Michael walked in. He was rubbing his eyes and squinting.

I said, "Welcome back! What's wrong with your eyes?"

He said, "Hi, honey. I don't know what happened, but when I turned into our driveway I saw a piercing flash of light."

"Oh," I said. "That must have been from the sun reflecting off the mirrors I placed around the fruit trees out front."

"I don't understand what you just said."

"Guess what! I changed our house all around to enhance the energy flow and attract happiness and prosperity into our lives."

"Oh, great," he said. "But first, I've got to tell you what happened during this business trip."

"Not before you see the giant rock in our bedroom," I said, leading him through the kitchen.

"I didn't understand what you said that time either."

"You need to see the giant rock I put in our bedroom," I said loudly and slowly, as if he were deaf. Why was this so hard to understand?

He said, "No, really, me first. Thursday, I was at this meeting and nothing was going right. My cell phone had no reception, I told my clients to come to the wrong address, my cab broke down, everything went wrong. The clients said they had no interest in working with me. Then this morning, everything started to change. And by noon I had landed the account. I've never seen such a complete turnaround in my life."

I said, "I know exactly why that happened."

He speculated, "Do you think it's because of my personality—you know, my ability to win people over?"

"Of course not. It's because I had a giant rock put in our bedroom and painted it red."

He stared at me. Then he said, "Honey, try lifting your arms and sticking out your tongue at the same time."

"I'm not having a stroke," I said irritably. "Come into the front hall. I moved our bed in here, so the chi energy of the house can't escape. It's feng shui. That's why you had such a great meeting."

"You mean you used feng shui to change our house around, and you think that's why my meeting went well?"

"Well, of course. I made all these changes this morning and was done by noon. Don't you think that's a bit of a coincidence?"

"Maybe you're on to something here."

Several hours later, we got into bed and fell asleep right away.

Suddenly the front door opened and hit our bed. We both woke up, startled. My neighbor slid in sideways through the door.

"Sorry it took me so long. I finally found my blood pressure cuff. So any dizziness, shortness of breath?"

"You don't realize that I used feng shui to change the physical health and well-being area on our bagua map, which would make it virtually impossible for me to have a stroke right now."

"Just give me your arm," she snapped.

I guess I'll have to work on the friendship and relationship area on my bagua map. Some people just don't get it.

32

The Woman with the Angelina Jolie Lips

Michael and I were watching an awards show one evening and saw Angelina and Brad walk up the red carpet. I said, "Gosh, I'd love to look like Angelina Jolie."

Michael said, "Well, she is very beautiful," trying his best to sound noncommittal.

After seeing an infomercial for the Amazing Lip Enlarging Lip Gloss for the fifty-fourth time, I decided to give it a try. It arrived by mail the promised eight weeks later.

I put some on one evening before Michael came home. It took about five minutes for me to see some results, but I thought my lips looked a little poutier, a little sexier, and I was pleased.

When Michael arrived, I showed off my new lips to him. "Gosh, they do look a little swollen."

"Really?" I quizzed. "Great!"

Michael picked up the lip gloss tube and said, "There's an emergency number on here. I wonder what that's for."

"Oh, it's probably just a number for reordering the lip gloss."

That weekend we went to a party at our neighbor's house. As I joined a group of women, one said, "Lauren, you look different. What have you done? You look great!"

"Well," I replied, "I'm wearing the Amazing Lip Enlarging Lip Gloss. It kind of stings, but I think it's worth it to have plumper lips."

Everyone totally agreed.

"I'd love to try some of your lip stuff if you don't mind," one friend said.

"So would I," said another.

We all trooped into the master bathroom and stood at the mirror, applying the Amazing Lip Enlarging Lip Gloss like a bunch of teenagers.

When we went back to the party, we all had plumper lips.

Our husbands thought it was great, and, believe it or not, some couples even started kissing.

The trouble didn't begin until thirty minutes later, when one of the husbands complained that his lips wouldn't stop itching. What a whiner! On another man's neck a red welt was beginning to form. Of course, the men started to panic.

More and more of the husbands started to complain. We finally figured out it was the Amazing Lip Enlarging Lip Gloss. The men were about to call the paramedics, when Michael remembered the number on the side of the tube.

I went into the kitchen, called the number, and a woman answered, "Amazing Lip Enlarging Lip Gloss hotline, can I help you?"

"I have twenty people here with welts all over their faces and necks. We think it's your lip gloss."

"Oh, for heaven's sakes, just try putting some butter on it, and you'll be fine. This happens all the time, don't get excited."

"Don't get excited?" I asked. "The people here hate me. This has lawsuit written all over it."

"Didn't you read our disclaimer in *Field and Stream*? We aren't responsible for any rashes, swelling, or skin rot of any kind." She hung up.

I grabbed a couple of sticks of butter out of the refrigerator and raced back to the party.

"I have the antidote," I announced, "and it's butter!"

Everyone applied the butter and the excitement was over.

As we were lying in bed that night, Michael said, "Do you still want to look like Angelina Jolie?"

"No, I've decided it would be easier for you to just look like Brad Pitt."

"No problem. I can match his lips any day."

33

The Designer Uncle Who Insists on a Biedermeier Master Bedroom for Caroline's Barbie House

Michael," I said, "I'm worried about your brother."

"Why, what's wrong?"

"Since he decided he wanted to present Caroline with a Barbie house for the holidays, he's been obsessed."

"He's not obsessed! It's just that when David decided to go into interior design, he wanted to do something for Caroline."

"But he keeps referring to Barbie as his 'client.' Since Mario Buatta took him on as a protégé and they worked together on the Kips Bay Showhouse, it seems he's had a little difficulty distinguishing between fantasy and reality."

"Well, you know that was a big project for him: he just adores Mario."

"Yes, but Barbie has been living in a shoebox for the past three years, and now she needs terrazzo tile for her entryway? And she needs them cut into one-half-inch pieces at the cost of $125 an hour by a tile setter?"

"Well, he said it's his treat for Caroline. Besides, he can

get everything wholesale. My only complaint is that he's put on the work schedule for me to re-grout Barbie's master bathroom floor next Friday. And I don't think it matters that much to Barbie."

"See, now you're doing it, too. You're talking about Barbie as if she's real."

"I just want her to like her new house," he said softly, as if he were Ty Pennington and Barbie were getting a new house from *Extreme Makeover*.

Later that day, David walked in after spending the day picking out window treatments for Barbie's house. He had been explaining to Caroline something about swags and jabots.

"Oh, David, I finished the needlepoint rug for the Barbie house guest bedroom. Do you like it?" I asked while proudly showing him the rug, which measured three by four *inches*.

"Oh, my goodness, Lauren," he said. "Didn't you get last night's memo?"

"What memo?"

"I sent out a memo to everyone last night saying that I was changing the color scheme in the guest bedroom."

"Why can't you just use this?"

"Lauren, you wouldn't want to compromise the integrity of this project. This is *so* important for Barbie. The flooring contractors are just finishing up the kitchen floor so let's go see how it looks."

As we looked at the floor in the kitchen of Barbie's house, David gasped. "Oh, this will never work at all. I thought I'd put laminate flooring in the kitchen since it's such a high-traffic area, but I can tell right now what's going to happen. When Barbie walks on this floor, her high heels will click too loudly."

He told the contractors they'd need to remove the laminate and that he'd come down to the store to pick out something else. They looked at each other and left.

"Now," he said briskly. "I think Barbie would want a chair rail in the dining room. We can mix Hepplewhite and Sheridan chairs, but not Chippendale. And we certainly don't want to do something post-Victorian. No one is doing Edwardian anymore. The primitive thing was over ten years ago."

I said, "I've heard red accent walls are really in right now."

David pretended not to hear me. "I had a client meeting with Caroline and Barbie yesterday. Caroline picked out Mission furniture. She must have Michael's taste for home decorating—everyone knows Mission furniture would never work in a Victorian house."

"David, Caroline is four years old."

"She already has a very good eye for color, though! I only hope the color swatches of fabric arrive in the next day or two so she can choose the colors for the master bedroom. Otherwise, I won't have time to order fabric to reupholster the furniture before Christmas."

"Order fabric? The color swatches of fabric themselves will be enough to cover all of the furniture."

He continued, "I thought we'd do a Biedermeier-styled master bedroom. If it was good enough for Napoleon, it should also work for Barbie."

Another week of time-consuming details, and the Barbie house was done and Caroline loved it.

After the holidays, as David was leaving for the airport, he said to us, "You know, on average, people redecorate their houses every five years, so call me when she's ready."

"Caroline?"

"No, Barbie. I just couldn't believe how easy it was to work with her. She was a delight! Maybe I could find some pieces when I go to Italy this spring."

Michael nodded. "Barbie would *love* that."

David practically skipped down the front sidewalk.

Now if we could only convince Barbie to keep her own house clean. But then again, not very many people with Biedermeier bedrooms do their own cleaning.

34

The Athletic Mom Who Is Lifting Weights Every Day at Ten a.m. While I Am Gaining Weight Every Day at Ten a.m.

I've never understood the Athletic Mom. Oh, sure, I exercise. I walk to the refrigerator and back many times a day.

Caroline's school has a bike rally every year to raise money. You donate forty dollars to bike forty miles and donate fifteen dollars to bike fifteen miles. When I first read this, I was stunned. You donate *more* money and then have to ride your bike *farther*. Shouldn't it be the other way around? Wouldn't you donate more money in order to bike *less*? Or pay forty dollars and just show up and have a barbecue. Or if physical exertion must take place, have a cakewalk. Get it, a *cake-*walk? Why not pay forty dollars and walk around a circle and get a cake at the end? Doesn't this sound better to you? Obviously, my input is desperately needed in the fund-raising committees at school.

Nevertheless, I decided I should think about getting into shape. Another mom told me about a yoga class she was taking and loving. She invited me to try it out.

When I showed up for the class that next week, I noticed

all of the women wore skintight leotards and had not one-eighth of an inch of excess flab. Their stomachs were not only flat, they were concave. Their makeup was perfect, their hair was perfect, their nails were perfect. Did I mention it was eight in the morning? Obviously, I left.

So I decided to try one of the 847 cable channels we pay for every month but never watch. I found *Yoga with Brandy,* which I hoped might be a cooking show, but unfortunately was an exercise show. There was Brandy, looking great in her skintight black leotard, with two other great-looking workout people, on the beach in front of the ocean. I looked around the room. What was missing? Let me see—oh, I've got it—the ocean. I couldn't possibly be expected to do yoga without an ocean.

Next, I tried the Pilates channel. Shawna and friends looked about the same as Brandy and her sidekicks, and she also had an ocean. I complained to another friend.

"Why don't you just take an aerobic walking class?" she asked. "I just started a new one that you could join."

"Well, I suppose . . ." I said doubtfully.

"It'll be fine," she said. "You'll love it. But first, what kind of athletic running shoes do you own?"

"The kind where you put them on and start running."

"Do they have stride sensors?"

"What are stride sensors?"

"I thought that everyone has at least one pair of running shoes with stride sensors. Where did you buy your running shoes?"

"Wal-Mart, I think." I shrugged.

"Wal-Mart?" she said incredulously. "Wal-Mart doesn't carry running shoes with stride sensors."

"You're probably right."

"Well, you need to replace your running shoes every five hundred miles. How long have you had yours?"

"I believe I bought them when I was a junior in college, which would be about eighteen years ago. See, they're right here," I said, pointing to my shoes in the closet.

"That's odd, they look brand-new."

"Yeah, well." I shrugged.

She turned back to me. "What pedometer do you currently own?"

"I don't have one."

"Okay, then, before we start, you need to buy the Sport-Brain iStep XII pedometer. You can download the data to the Internet and it will graph your distance, speed, and caloric output."

And to think I used to worry that people could only gain access to my credit card information over the Internet.

"But what if I don't want a graph charting my caloric output?" I complained. I wondered if the term "flatliner" meant anything to her.

"Well, of course you want to chart your caloric output. Now let's go over the basics of walking."

"The basics of walking?"

"Most people don't know how to walk."

"Well, I have been walking without any problems for about forty-seven years now. But okay, tell me how to walk."

She cleared her throat and started talking as if she were reciting something from memory. "Walking is done in a rolling motion. First, you strike the ground with your heel. Then you roll through the step from heel to toe. Then you push off with your toe. And then you bring the back leg forward to strike again with the heel."

I tried it and fell over.

"No, no, no," she said impatiently. "Let's go over it again."

The next time I fared better. I made it to the couch and back.

"See," she said triumphantly. "I knew you could do it."

We promised to meet to walk the next morning and she left. I was pleased. I wondered how high my caloric output level had been during the excursion to the couch and back. Surely it must have been enough to cover the three chocolate chip cookies that were left in the kitchen.

So far, my decision to get into shape was working out pretty well.

35

The Perfect Halloween Mom Who Carves Forty-three Pumpkins in the Image of the U.S. Presidents

Naturally, I was running late for Caroline's autumn party at school. Luckily, I had been the first one to notice the sign-up sheet regarding what to bring, and put my name down under "paper plates." The unfortunate moms who don't stay alert and watch for the sign-up sheet often end up having to bring items such as cookies decorated with bats or other time-consuming treats. I, however, like to stay alert in this department.

As I was walking in from the parking lot, an overachieving mom was returning to her car. "Oh, hi, Melinda," I greeted her. "Are you leaving so soon?"

"Oh, no," she said happily. "This is my fourth trip back to my U-Haul. I had so much to bring for the party, it's taken me a while to get it all in."

"U-Haul?" I asked.

"Yes, that's it over there," she said pointing across the parking lot. "I rented a U-Haul to bring everything here for the party. I needed it for the forty-three pumpkins I carved."

"Forty-three pumpkins?"

"I carved the faces of all forty-three presidents into pumpkins. Since I am in charge of the autumn party this year, I thought I'd try and combine it with U.S. history." I vaguely remembered that Melinda had been a history major at Stanford. "I've always thought you can learn so much about history through the use of produce."

"I've always thought that, too," I said nonchalantly, hoping she didn't realize I was being sarcastic.

She continued. "Actually, would you mind helping me? I've already brought in George Washington through James Monroe. I'll take Buchanan and Cleveland. If you could grab William Howard Taft, that would be great," she said, pointing at an enormous pumpkin.

"Why is Taft so much larger than the others?" I asked.

"Because Taft weighed over 350 pounds, of course. Once he gave up his seat on a streetcar, and three women were able to sit down."

"I didn't know that. I can't believe all the work you've put into this."

"Yes, I started back in September. I had to buy three extra refrigerators for my garage to store them. And let me tell you, it wasn't easy, especially carving all the curls on George Washington and John Adams."

"Wow."

"In the glove compartment," she continued, "are historically correct wire-rim eyeglasses for Teddy Roosevelt, Woodrow Wilson, and Harry Truman. I tried to use smaller pumpkins for them so the glasses would fit. It's funny, but no antique shop I checked had glasses large enough to fit pumpkins. I finally found some on eBay."

A few more moms walked up and offered to help.

Melinda gave out the instructions: "Okay, Michelle, you grab Pierce and Fillmore. Ellen, you grab Tyler and Jefferson."

Michelle said hesitantly, "I'm not sure how to tell which ones are Pierce and Fillmore."

"Oh, for heaven's sakes," Melinda said with irritation, "you obviously don't know much about the presidents. Everyone knows that Pierce was the best-looking president—even Harry Truman said that."

Michelle said hesitantly again, "And which of these pumpkins is the best-looking?"

Melinda stood above the Pierce pumpkin and pointed down at it. "It's *this* one," she said irritably.

The other moms averted their eyes.

Ellen retorted, "Well, Truman said that only because John Kennedy hadn't been president yet. I think he was the best-looking, and I'm taking him in."

Michelle said, "No, I'm taking him in."

"I said first," Ellen said, grabbing John Kennedy and running to the door. I thought to myself that this is exactly what happens when women with young kids haven't had sex for a while.

I turned to Melinda and said, "You've certainly outdone yourself this time."

"Yes," she said wearily, "this has been much more difficult than I had planned. Some of the presidents were extremely difficult to do. I know that Lincoln was one of the greatest presidents, but he was definitely the most difficult to carve. Can you imagine? The angles in his face, the mole, the unsightly beard. No wonder his wife went nuts. People should consider these things when determining presidential greatness. At this point, he's definitely off my list. In fact, he didn't turn out that well. I think I'll just leave him in the car."

As Michelle and I followed her in with the remaining pumpkins, I felt sorry for Lincoln. All that work: the exact timing of the Emancipation Proclamation, the simple eloquence of the Gettysburg Address, the daunting task of keeping the Union together. All that, just to one day be left in the car.

36

The Wine Connoisseur Woman Whose Wine Rests More Than I Do

At a recent party, I was talking to Jennifer, a woman I had known in school. Her husband walked into the living room where we were talking and said, "Our host asked us to taste this wine and tell him what we think."

Jennifer replied, "Is it a reserva? I thought we were supposed to taste a reserva."

"No, I just tasted this wine and it can't possibly be a reserva. I detected a hint of oak when I tasted this wine, so it was probably stored in an oak barrel for a few weeks." He paused. "Oh, I saw someone in the kitchen who I wanted to speak to about a new contract at work. I'll be right back." He left the wine with us.

Jennifer poured wine into each of our glasses.

I drank all of mine and lifted my glass and said, "Tasted good to me!"

"No, no, no, Lauren," said Jennifer. "First you must 'nose' the wine and notice the delicate aromas. Then you must swirl the wine in the glass, let it rest, and then nose the wine again, whereby you will then notice an absolutely profound difference in the aroma. Here, let's try it."

She poured more wine into my glass.

"Okay now, remember, nose the wine, swirl, rest, nose again."

I sat down on the couch and drank up all the wine in the glass.

She said, "What are you doing?"

"I'm resting. Didn't you say I needed to rest?"

"No," she said, "I said to let the *wine* rest."

"Why would the wine need to rest? I'm the one who vacuumed my whole house today."

"Oh, for heaven's sakes," she said. "Here, let me pour you more wine," she said, pouring more wine into my glass.

She continued, "Okay, let's go over this again. First nose the wine, swirl, rest, nose again."

"What do you mean, 'nose the wine'?" I asked. "Do you mean that I need to drink it so fast that it sloshes up against my nose?"

"No, it means to *smell* it," she said impatiently.

"Why didn't you just say that?"

"Okay, let's try it again. Nose the wine, swirl, rest, nose again."

I smelled the wine, rested on the couch, and drank up the wine in my glass.

"No, no, no, you were supposed to nose the wine, *swirl,* rest, and then nose again."

"I did. I smelled the wine, rested, and drank it."

"No, no, no," she said again impatiently. "You never 'smell' a wine. You 'nose' it."

"You shouldn't say 'nose' it, rather you should say that

I 'know' it." I walked over and opened a window, as it was really getting hot in there.

She poured some more wine for me. "Okay, first, nose the wine. Let's see you do that."

I sloshed the wine up against my nose and then drank it.

"Now what?" I asked, sitting down on the couch again. I called out loudly to the other room, *"Could someone in there bring me a pillow?"*

"Oh, my God, I've never seen anything like this. I'm going to try this one more time. Nose the wine, swirl, rest, and then nose it again." She poured me more wine.

"If it's all she same to you, I don't feel much like twirling."

"I didn't say 'twirl,' I said 'swirl.'"

"Well, that makes even less sense." I drank all the wine in the glass. *"Hey, where's my pillow?"* I called out to the other room.

"Okay, I'm going to try this once more. Nose, swirl, rest, nose." She poured me more wine.

I drank the wine. *"I'm really going to need a pillow in here,"* I hollered at the people in the other room.

Her husband walked into the room.

"Where's my pillow?" I asked him.

He said, "When I was in the kitchen I thought I heard someone yelling for a pillow, but I didn't know it was you."

I replied, "You mean you didn't *nose* it was me."

"What?" he said blankly.

"Do you guys think it's hot in here?"

"No."

I yawned. "Well, I guess I'll call it a night. I'm going to bed."

"But you don't live here," she said.

"What's your point?" I asked. I wandered off, found a bed upstairs, and crawled into it. Now, if only the room would stop twirling. Or swirling. Whatever.

37

The Woman Who Puts All Her Photographs into an Album the Same Day She Gets Them Back

One afternoon, just as I was getting ready to finish off the dessert I had made a few hours earlier, the phone rang.

"Lauren, this is Peggy at Photo I. How are you?"

"Fine, Peggy. What's wrong?" I knew her casually, but I couldn't imagine her calling just to chat.

She whispered loudly, "I'm calling to let you know that the store owner is getting ready to clean out all the photos that have been left here for several years. You have eleven packages. They appear to be of Christmas, Thanksgiving, Halloween, your trip to Disneyland, the Fourth of July, and your vacation at the lake."

"How embarrassing," I thought to myself. I said, "Thank you so much, Peggy. I'll be in tomorrow by noon."

"Oh, and I just found some Easter pictures of yours, too, but I don't know which year."

"I'm only one woman," I joked. "I can't be expected to do everything."

"Right!" she said and hung up.

Standing in line at the photo shop, I saw a woman I had met in a cooking class. We had been friendly and had been meaning to get together and have coffee one day. She said, "I know this is spur of the moment, but why don't you come over now if you have time?"

"Great," I replied. "I have over an hour before I need to pick up Caroline, so that would work out well."

I followed her to her house, which was nearby. As soon as the coffee was brewing she led me into her family room, where she began to place her new photos into volume twelve of her twenty-four-volume leather-bound set of albums.

"I hope you will excuse me, but I really like to get photos properly placed immediately. You know how it is," she graciously apologized.

"Oh, yes," I lied, as my method was somewhat different. I would leave my pictures strewn out on the countertop. Then as they began to get sticky with orange juice after a few days, I would throw them in a shoebox where they could never be found or separated again.

"Take your time," I said and began to walk around the room.

On the walls of the family room were photos of her four daughters dressed up for the holidays with adorable coordinating outfits. And then I noticed the beautiful dance recital pictures of each of the girls, perfectly lit and unhurried. Charming. At Caroline's last recital, I forgot to take pictures until we were on our way home, but I did get a good picture of her in the backseat of the car.

As we sat down in the kitchen to have coffee, I spotted a wall series of adorable hand-painted frames entitled FIRST DAY OF SCHOOL FIRST GRADE, FIRST DAY OF SCHOOL SECOND GRADE, and so on. Each was filled with a child's snapshot posed in front of the same back door. Each girl's lunch box coordinated perfectly with her outfit. I felt slightly sick.

Then, as I sat at the kitchen counter drinking my coffee, I saw, to my dismay, that the Photo Mom had her Christmas card order form ready with several fabulous proofs waiting (it was only September). They showed her entire family in coordinating Christmas outfits with perfectly matching hair decorations. Even the dog had a coordinating ribbon around his neck. The ornaments on the tree, the wrapping paper on the presents, and the girls' dresses all matched.

As I commented on how nice these pictures were, the Photo Mom said, "Well, it is rather a pain to put up our Christmas tree in July to get our Christmas photos done, but I hate to wait until the last minute."

"Oh, I do, too," I sighed. "You put up your tree in July?" I felt sick again.

"Yes, I take it right down again and then put it up again at Thanksgiving."

My mind drifted back to last year when I had to use an Easter picture of Caroline for the holiday cards since I had run out of time to do anything else. I had really tried to get the three of us together for a picture, but the only clothes that I could find for us that matched were Bronco T-shirts and jeans. Somehow, that wasn't the look I was going for.

Suddenly, I remembered one Christmas when I was in high school and my mother sent out a lovely picture of herself and the dog in front of our Christmas tree. In the card she explained that she had forgotten to tell the rest of the family about the appointment with the photographer.

Genetics do explain a lot.

38

The Husband Who Asks You Every Day, "Can You Call Someone About That?"

According to the *International Journal of Male Brain Structure,* a particularly annoying aspect of the husband brain structure is how it triggers him to to repeat over and over, "Can you call someone about that?" It doesn't matter what you are talking about.

For example, you are discussing your upcoming trip to Disneyland. You have the tickets in your hand. He says to you, "Can you call the airline and confirm the reservation?"

And you say, "But I have the tickets right here in my hand."

And he says to you, "Well, I still think you'd better call."

Then you say, "Well, if you're worried about it, why don't you call?"

And then he shrugs his shoulders and walks away, because the point wasn't really to check the reservations, the point was that he wanted you to call someone because of an irrational need triggered by the husband brain structure to have you spend your time in unnecessary and mindless ways.

Your car is in the shop. They said it would be ready Thursday. It is now only Tuesday. He says to you, "Why don't you call and see how the car is coming along?"

You say, "Well, they said they would have it done on Thursday. We know what's wrong with it. They are fixing what's wrong with it. So I see no need to call them."

And he says, "Well, I still think you'd better call."

And you say, "Well, if you're worried about it, why don't you call?"

And he shrugs his shoulders and walks away, because the point wasn't really to see how the car was coming along, the point was that he wanted you to call someone because of an irrational need sparked by the husband brain to have you spend your time in unnecessary and mindless ways.

He's rushed a suit of his to the cleaners and it's supposed to be ready for him to pick up the next day. Late that afternoon, he says, "Why don't you call and make sure my suit will be ready to pick up tomorrow?"

And you say, "Didn't you tell me it would be ready tomorrow?"

And he says, "Yes, but I think you'd better call and find out if it really will be ready tomorrow."

And you say, "Well, if you're worried about it, why don't you call?"

And he shrugs his shoulders and walks away, because the point wasn't really to see how the clothes were coming along, the point was that he wanted you to call someone because of an irrational need spurred by the husband brain structure to have you spend your time in unnecessary and mindless ways.

Of course, I could give you at least another forty-seven examples of this off the top of my head, but you get the picture—and I have no need to make you spend your time in unnecessary and mindless ways.

39

The Woman Who Goes Twice a Week to the Elitist Car Wash

Gosh, Stacy, your car always looks so clean," I commented to another mom while we were waiting for our kids to come out of school.

"Oh, I go to the Lavage de Voiture. Have you been there? It's an *experience*."

"What does Lavage de Voiture mean in English?"

"Car wash." She shrugged.

"Well, maybe I'll try it out after I pick up Caroline."

Stacy said, "You might want to change your clothes before you go. And have your nails done. And maybe some highlights in your hair."

"Oh," I said, "right."

Several days later, after I had my nails and hair done, I pulled up to the Lavage de Voiture. Two male attendants all in white sprinted out to greet me. I left my car in their care and walked into the waiting room where about half a dozen perfectly coiffed women sat.

An elderly gentleman wearing a gray-striped morning coat

approached me. "I'm Hubert, your maitre d'," he said with an English accent. "Would you like a glass of champagne?"

"Oh, well, okay."

"And would you like an hors d'oeuvre? Our chef just took a tray of lobster in pastry shells out of the oven." He bent down with a beautiful tray of delectable appetizers that looked wonderful.

"Yes, thank you," I said, taking three of the shells because I had only had a small breakfast of pancakes, eggs, and sausage that morning.

Hubert continued, "And here's a selection of magazines for your enjoyment. Would you like the *New Yorker*, the *Atlantic Monthly,* or *Harper's*?"

I asked, "You don't have anything like *Family Circle,* do you?"

Just then a long-legged blond walked in.

"Oh, *Hubert,* how *are* you?" she exclaimed. "Today is the *day* for those *yummy* lobster treats, isn't it?"

"Yes, madame, and how good to see you. I'll go to the kitchen immediately and have the chef cut one up for you. I know you only like to eat a quarter of a lobster pastry shell."

"Well, I must keep myself in shape, mustn't I?" she exclaimed.

I looked down at the three pastry shells on my plate.

"And would you like your usual low-carb energy drink, Mrs. Erlhoeffer?

"Oh, Hubert, you're such a darling. Thank you so much."

I started to eat my lobster shells. They were the most exquisite appetizers I had ever tasted.

At that point I realized that the blond was staring at something on my blouse, which of course, was part of a pastry shell. I realized at that point that I was probably going to spill more on myself than she was going to eat.

Just then we all heard a loud, screeching sound. After a few seconds someone announced over the loudspeaker, "Mrs. Perry, would you come to the front? The bumper has fallen off your car."

Everyone looked around the room, eager to see who would claim the bumperless car. I rose and said, "I have to use the restroom," and proceeded to the front.

A mechanic greeted me at the door and said in a loud voice, "I've never seen anything like it. Was your bumper loose before coming here?"

"Not that I know of," I stammered, trying to make him back up into another room that would be out of earshot. It's too bad the HIPA confidentiality laws that pertain to the health-care system don't also apply to your car.

He said, "Well, I'll tie it up the best I can. It'll be done in a few minutes."

A person sitting behind a glass desk said, "You can pay now if you'd like, Mrs. Perry."

"Oh, yes, of course," I said. I dug into my purse and handed her a twenty-dollar bill.

"Is this the tip?" she asked.

"No," I stammered again, "it's, you know, the payment."

"Oh, Mrs. Perry, it's $74.95 to have your car washed here."

"Oh, of course," I said, trying not to let me pupils enlarge too much. "I'll have to give you my credit card."

"Very good, Mrs. Perry," she said, taking my card. "You can return to the waiting room for a few minutes while we tidy everything up for you."

"Yes, I, well, okay," I said and returned to the other room.

After I had sat there for a few minutes enjoying the rest of my lobster shells, someone came on the loudspeaker again: "Mrs. Perry, your credit card has been declined. Again, Mrs. Perry, your credit card has been declined. Can you please return to the front desk?"

I stood up and with a weak laugh said, "That champagne ran right through me! I'm off to the bathroom again!"

I approached the woman at the glass desk. "I just can't understand it. I'll call my husband and have him give you his number." After calling Michael, everything was straightened out.

A few days later the estimate for fixing the bumper came back from the mechanic. Let's see:

Manicure: $30.00

Hair color and style: $140.00

Bumper repair: $695.00

Getting the car washed: $94.95 ($74.95 plus a $20 tip)

Eating three exquisite lobster shells: Priceless

I've already started saving up to go back.

40

The Woman Who Knows the Difference Between "High Tea" and "Low Tea"

My neighbor Elizabeth and I recently were invited to a "high tea" party in our neighborhood. She sounded anxious on the phone.

"Have you ever been to high tea before?"

I said, "Well, actually, no I haven't."

"I'd better approve your attire ahead of time. You can't breeze in there wearing just anything."

"No, of course not. I thought I'd wear this beautiful linen pantsuit I just purchased."

"*Pants!* Pants will never work! This is *high* tea, not *low* tea."

"What should I wear?"

"What did you wear to your own wedding?"

"A long white wedding dress."

"Just take it down a notch from that and you'll be fine."

Finally, the day of the big tea arrived. I was thrilled when we were seated at a lovely table.

Some time later, after the food had been passed, I was about to take a bite of a tiny sandwich, when Elizabeth whispered loudly in my ear, "You don't start with the sandwich, you start with the scone. Then you have the sandwich and then the dessert!"

"Oh, okay," I said, dropping the sandwich as if it were filled with shaved lead instead of chicken salad.

I took the small pitcher of cream and poured some into my tea.

"You don't put the Devonshshire cream in your tea. You dab the Devonshire cream on the scone after you've put on the jam!" she whispered emphatically.

"Oh, sorry," I whispered back. "What should I do with my tea now that the cream is in there?"

"You'd better drink it before someone sees it in there."

I downed my cup of tea.

After finishing my scone, I popped a tiny sandwich in my mouth.

Elizabeth looked anxiety-stricken, as if I had just placed my leg up on the table. She whispered, "You never eat an entire sandwich at once! Rather, you take tiny bites of it!"

I said, "But it's only an eighth of an inch. I can hardly see it, let alone divide it up."

"That doesn't matter. Do you want the hostess to ask us to leave?"

That sounded pretty good right now, although I still hadn't had dessert. I took a one-thirty-second-of-an-inch bite of my "sandwich." Then I took a drink of my newly poured creamless tea.

Elizabeth whispered again, "You never drink tea that way. I was going to say something before, but you were doing so many other things wrong. You must hold the cup and saucer up to your chest, *and then* take the teacup off the saucer and take a sip of the tea. *But never ever* just take the cup off the saucer while it's sitting on the table."

"Oh, okay." I began to worry that I might develop some kind of anxiety disorder by the time we were done.

I took another drink of tea after first taking the cup and saucer up to my chest. Since the tea was hot, I blew delicately on it a little bit.

Elizabeth began to clutch her chest. "I can't believe you just did that!" she whispered loudly.

"No blowing on the tea?"

"Oh—my—God."

I decided the tea needed something. I asked her to pass the sugar cubes.

"Now whatever you do," she instructed, "do not let the sugar tongs dip down into your tea."

"Oh, right." I carefully dropped a sugar cube in my tea, but because I was holding the tongs so high, the cube dropping into the cup splashed the tea all over my dress.

Elizabeth began to hyperventilate. She grabbed her purse and began digging around. "I know I have some Xanax in here," she said between breaths. She found a few pills and popped them in her mouth.

That night I had nightmares that I drank the Devonshire cream straight from the little pitcher and that I forced Elizabeth to eat an entire plate of tiny sandwiches all at once. I couldn't wait to see the expression on a therapist's face upon learning that I needed treatment for post-traumatic stress disorder because of a tea party. But as I called around,

I actually found several therapists who specialize in stress disorders resulting from high tea. With intense treatment, they predicted the nightmares should stop in about five or six years, but that I couldn't attend any tea parties with Elizabeth until then. It'll be hard, but I guess my mental health and well-being will have to come first.

41

The Perfect Stage Mom Who Wants the Kindergarten Class to Perform *The Bitter Tears of Petra Von Kant*

While in kindergarten, Caroline decided that she wanted to perform in the annual kindergarten play, and since no other moms except for one had signed up, I decided to volunteer. I anticipated how cute Caroline would look possibly in a little red riding costume, or maybe playing Little Bear or the fox in a play adapted from a Maurice Sendak children's book.

On the first day of rehearsal, we all made our way to the front of the theater and sat down. The stage director, the other volunteer mom, was standing on the stage. She began, "I'm so glad you're all here today. I have directed plays both on and off Broadway. I'm new to directing actors at this age level, but I'm sure we'll be fine. I've decided to let all of you choose which play you'd like to perform. Since there are only about ten of you, I was thinking we could do *The Bitter Tears of Petra Von Kant*."

I looked at the group. One of the boys was picking his nose.

"Since you're not jumping at that one, what about *Jacques*

Brel Is Alive and Well and Living in Paris? It's a wonderful play which celebrates the songs of French composer Brel, with a diverse blend of boleros and tangos."

She continued, "This play is good in that it explores the nuances of life and death, but never forgetting that life, in the midst of its sorrow and pain, reveals much mirth."

Several of the "actors" began opening the snacks their mothers had packed for them.

The Perfect Stage Director Mom went on, "Before we decide, I should really get a little information from you. How many of you have ever seen *The Iliad: Book I* either on or off Broadway?"

One girl started doing backward flips in the aisle.

"No one? I think that something within this particular genre might work, although the antagonist and the protagonist are not closely aligned. And, of course, a play such as this would require a neutral density filter, with which I doubt this theater is equipped. We should probably do something which contains a performative, you know, which is understandable only within a matrix that is social and semiotic at the same time."

One of the girls said in a loud voice, "I cut my finger today playing in the sandbox. Does anyone want to see it?"

All of the "actors" ran over to take a look.

"That's nothing," said another voice. "I once gashed my head open and had fourteen stitches."

In a louder voice I heard, "I once had twenty stitches!"

Still louder, "I had thirty!"

"Really?" they all chorused in amazement.

"Yeah, I fell off a trampoline onto a rock. It was really cool! Do you want to see my scar?"

159

They all crowded around him and yelled in unison, "You're so lucky! Lucky, lucky, lucky!"

"Class, class," she exclaimed. "I need your attention. It seems that you're saying you'd like to do a more physically intense play. We could do *The Last Word,* a play about the character Henry Grunewald, a Viennese Jew who fled Germany during World War II. In fact, that play is about to open off Broadway. Wouldn't it be fun if we could all fly to New York and go? The tickets to the play are cheap—I believe they're in the sixty- to seventy-dollar range. And then of course there's airfare and hotel costs. Lauren, how much money do we have in our theater fund?"

I cleared my throat. "Three dollars and fifty-seven cents."

She looked crestfallen.

I continued, "As enticing as it sounds to take a group of six-year-olds to New York and see a play about the Nazi regime, why don't we just focus on the play we're going to do?"

She continued anyway with the Nazi theme. "What about *Radio Mirth and the Third Reich,* which is a depiction of how the Golden Age of radio distracted the world as the Germans swept their way through Europe?"

I said, "I think something lighter might be good."

She thought for a few seconds. "I've got it! What about *My Mother's Italian, My Father's Jewish and I'm in Therapy!* That's a wonderful, light play. I just love the part of Uncle Vito."

I looked around the room. I began calculating that if I flung my body from the stage into the orchestra pit I might be hurt badly enough to be out for the entire play.

I think I'll try it. I just might get lucky, lucky, lucky.

42

The Woman Who Loses Weight Without Hanging Out at the Center for Infectious Disease Control

I was scanning a magazine at the grocery store checkout line when a headline caught my eye. It read, PARSLEY IS THE PERFECT ANYTIME FOOD.

Instantly, I became incensed. Everyone knows that dough-nuts are the perfect anytime food—breakfast, mid-morning snack, lunch, midnight . . . How many foods do you feel like eating anytime?

I returned home intent on sharing a good laugh with my husband over it. He, however, turned serious.

"You know, Lauren, this is probably not the time to bring up the subject of a diet, but we did promise ourselves we would start cutting back on January second and it is already the fifteenth."

Why hadn't I kept my big mouth shut?

He was on a roll now. "Remember how great Bill and San-dra Wells looked at the office Christmas party? They each lost fifteen pounds."

A few dietless days passed and I kept thinking how great

Sandra Wells had looked. Damn her. Fifteen pounds and new fake nails. I was so jealous. That could be me at the company summer picnic.

I made an appointment at the local diet center. I couldn't believe that I was actually going to pay someone to nag me about eating.

I entered through the glass doors warily. Everyone was smiling, helpful, and thin.

"Hi, I'm Joan. I'll be your personal counselor. Let me show you around. This is our 'Wall of Fame.' It's for before and after pictures."

I was surprised to see how successful these people had been. I even recognized a clerk at my local grocery store in one of the pictures.

"Step in my office and we can get started," Joan invited.

"Don't we meet in big groups?" I asked.

"Oh, no!" she exclaimed, horrified. "You are here for private consultation. Groups never work."

After I weighed in, she started filling out papers.

"Tell me, Lauren, what are your weight goals?" Joan smiled encouragingly.

"To look like Calista Flockhart." (These thin people need to get real. Doesn't everyone want to look like Calista Flockhart?)

"We find that people do better if they set attainable goals."

"So Calista is out of the question?"

"I'm afraid so." She nodded seriously.

We settled on my losing twenty pounds. Next, she left me alone to complete a "short survey about my diet lifestyle."

Eating Habits

Question: Of the four food groups, which is your favorite?
I wrote: Chocolate cake.

Question: Do you eat three meals a day?
I wrote: Minimum.

Question: Name your three favorite vegetables.
I wrote: Corn chips, potato chips, and cheese curls (which are made with partially hydrogenated *vegetable* oil, so I assume that counts).

Question: Do you have eight glasses of water per day?
I wrote: I don't think I've had eight glasses of water in the course of my entire life.

Question: Do you eat while you're driving?
I wrote: Besides putting on makeup, what else is there to do?

I bought a week's worth of frozen food. After Joan assured me that she had once been overweight herself, I felt encouraged.

When I ate the first dinner, however, it didn't satisfy me. I decided to try a different weight-loss center.

First, I went to Target to see if they had any home liposuction kits. They didn't. I kept watching the news for stem-cell research reports concerning thin upper arms, but nothing. I had often used prayer as a diet aid, but this time I went to a real church to pray for weight loss. Didn't lose an ounce.

I decided to try another program.

As I approached the clerk at the counter area, I noticed everyone was smiling, helpful, and thin. I was told to weigh in and then join the group in the auditorium.

"Don't I get any private counseling?" I inquired.

"Oh, no!" she exclaimed, horrified. "Private sessions never work."

After we had all settled in, the leader announced we would receive twenty points per day. There was a slide-rule calculator thing to calculate points. This was dangerously close to math, but maybe they had tutors.

When I returned home, I tried to calculate how many points I had already used up that day, so I'd know how much I could eat for dinner. I kept forgetting to carry a number, so I gave Michael a list of what I had eaten.

After adding it up he said, "How many points are you allowed each day?"

I replied, "Twenty."

"Well, I wouldn't plan on eating anything tonight."

"Why not?"

"You've already had 157 points today."

"Oh." I was crestfallen.

"And if you can't eat until today's points are worked off, you won't be able to eat until two months from now."

Things were looking rather bleak.

At the next meeting, people were invited to announce how their lives had improved. I announced that I had not lost any weight, but that my math skills were better. That's more than I could say two weeks ago.

43

The Conspiracy Among Men to Be Annoying Just Before You Have Company

If Woman #1 calls up Woman #2 and finds out that Woman #2 has out-of-town company arriving later that day, Woman #1 immediately says, "Never mind. I'll call you next week when they've left." Then she hangs up.

Not so with men. When men find out you have guests coming, it becomes their mission to consume as much of your time as they possibly can. They begin talking slowly, walking slowly—in fact, most of their major organs begin to shut down.

One evening before Michael's sister and her family arrived from out of town, I was frantically trying to clean up the house. There were dishes piled up in the sink, the kitchen floor hadn't been swept, the lightbulb by the front door was out, making it impossible to even *find* the door, and it goes without saying that the cat had just thrown up on the living-room carpet.

And then I saw Michael, sitting at the kitchen table, diligently working on something. I said, "What are you doing?"

He replied, "I'm just filling out a sweepstakes form. We could win a million dollars."

Every woman in America knows what I was thinking after he said *that*, so I don't need to repeat it here.

Here's another example of this annoying behavior: a friend of mine was getting ready to have a bridal shower for her favorite niece. She had prepared a beautiful lunch and placed rented tables throughout the living room. White linen tablecloths, sparkling crystal glasses, and fine off-white china had all been placed meticulously on the five round tables. Just as the first guests were arriving, her soot-covered husband walked into the front entryway and said to her, "You'll be glad to know that I just cleaned out the fireplace in the living room."

I don't need to tell you what she thought at that moment either, because all of you know what it was.

And then there was another friend of mine who had recently moved into a new house with her husband. A couple of weeks after they moved in, she was frantically trying to get ready to have guests stay with them. Nothing was ready—the bed hadn't even been set up in the guest bedroom, not to mention that the guest bathroom had no towels, no soap, no toilet paper, no anything.

A few hours before the guests were to arrive, my friend said to her husband, "I need help getting the bed set up in the guest bedroom."

"Oh," he replied. "I'm much too busy to help you with *that*."

"Why?" she asked. "What are you doing?"

"I'm busy replacing all the dimmer switches in the house."

Again, no need to report on what came next.

When you're in a hurry to get something done, there is a gene men possess that makes it possible for them to sense this, and then do everything they can to keep you from getting anything done. This is true for men of all ages. Even teenagers.

For example, on the day I'm expecting guests from out of town, I can always count on running into the "I'm in No Hurry to Go Anywhere" bagger at the supermarket.

I pay for my groceries and begin walking to the exit, assuming the grocery bagger is following behind me with my cart of groceries. When I reach the door, I turn around and see him standing back at the checkout lane, talking to a fellow bagger. I politely motion to him where I am, and he hollers, "I'll be right there."

I wait a little while and then go back to the checkout stand, where I find him discussing with another bagger whether my groceries show I am following the Atkins or the Zone diet.

My bagger says, "Tom here thinks you're on the Atkins Diet, but by the looks of this grocery cart, I'd say you're more of a Zone person."

"You know, I'm in a hurry here. Can we just go now?"

"I find the lack of carbs in your diet interesting," the bagger continues, "but you don't go overboard on protein either. I just can't figure it out."

"I'm on the Whatever I Can Make in Ten Minutes diet since I have company coming in less than an hour."

Undeterred, he says, "Recent studies show that cruciferous vegetables are extremely important as part of a healthy diet. I see no broccoli, brussels sprouts, or cauliflower in here."

"Look, I don't have time for this. Just follow me to my car." I turn and walk toward the door.

He begins following me, but when I get to the door, I realize I've lost him again. My grocery cart is now sitting by a wall, abandoned.

I go over to get it, and he comes out from a side hallway. "I had to put my coat on," he says, assuming control of the cart once again. "You don't want me catching cold, do you?"

I turn and hurry toward the door. He slowly walks behind me, as if he has just begun to regain consciousness after surgery.

I turn to him and say, "I'm really in a big hurry."

Ignoring this statement, he says, "I see you're buying Goo Gone. What do you need that for?"

"It's a long story. Can you walk any faster?"

He says, "My mother uses that to get price stickers off new dishes and it works very well. Purchased any new dishes lately?"

"I have, but that's not what I'm buying it for."

"Then how were you able to get the stickers off your new dishes? With most dishes, that's a difficult thing to do." He is strolling along as if enjoying a sunset on Maui.

We finally reach the outside of the store. I practically shout at him. *"I am in a hurry."*

"I'm moving as fast as I can, ma'am. Did you buy the dishes we have on sale? They're really nice."

"I didn't buy them here."

He stops walking. "Why not? Don't tell me the blue flowers

168

didn't work for you? As I understand it, they go with most other colors. Didn't you at least try to make them work?"

Right then something in me snaps. I grab him by his jacket and push him up against the wall of the store. I then take my grocery cart and run to my car. I get the trunk open, fling the groceries in as fast as I can, and slam the trunk shut. Seeing him heading my way, I aim the cart for him and push it in his direction as hard as I can. I then jump in my car. Before I know it, he taps on my car window. Thinking I might have injured him, I roll down the window.

He leans in and says, "You wanna see a sample of the blue dishes? I could go back in and get them and show them to you. I'm sure you'd really like them."

I push my foot against the gas pedal, so hard in fact that I'm standing almost straight up in the car. I can sense what it would feel like to be psychotic. He continues to talk at my window: "There's a nice little green stem, too." Finally, the engine turns over and I rev it up a few times, making sure it won't die. People begin to stare.

As I lurch the car forward, the engine dies. He runs forward alongside the car and says, "The pattern on the dishes is a little blue flower, like a little blue bachelor button."

I then lurch the car forward again and again as he runs beside me. Finally, I take off. As I look out my rearview mirror I see him running, trying to keep up with me as I tear out of the parking lot.

Above the roar of my engine, he shouts and waves, *"I'll put some dishes on hold for you. I know you're really going to like them."*

44

The Woman Who Never Loses Her Luggage When She Travels

I won a twenty-pound turkey from a school raffle one year. I packed the bird, which would feed twenty-five people, in my suitcase and took it with us to my in-laws' for Christmas.

We flew into Chicago Midway without any problems, even though I lied when I was asked whether we had anything perishable in our luggage. The turkey wasn't really perishable at that moment since it was frozen. It wouldn't start to become perishable until well after the flight, right?

Of course everyone's suitcase arrived promptly—except mine. We watched and waited, but no suitcase. Michael became worried when he realized my Christmas present for him was also in that suitcase.

While we were waiting for the representative in baggage claim to find out what had happened, I noticed a woman who was holding what appeared to be a GPS monitor. Curious, I asked her why she needed it.

"This is the only reliable way to know where my suitcase is at any given time. The airlines lost my luggage once and they told me it had gone on to Guam, but since I installed a computer chip in it, I was able to calculate the latitude and longitude of my suitcase and found that it was right outside on the tarmac. They went out and looked again, and sure enough, there it was. The start-up cost for a GPS for a suitcase is hefty, but it ends up being worth the expense."

This was a woman to be reckoned with.

Finally, a representative came out and told us that my suitcase had flown on to Idaho, but not to worry, they'd have it to me by the next morning. It was decided they would fly the suitcase to O'Hare, and then deliver it to my in-laws' home.

The next afternoon, when the turkey, I mean the suitcase, didn't arrive, I called the airline. "Oh, they always tell the poor fool it's going to arrive the next day," the airline representative laughed hysterically, "but it never does. Call sometime next week." She hung up.

"Next *week*?" I said, thinking of the E. coli poisoning that was about to spread across the United States when my suitcase made contact with other luggage.

Very early the next morning the phone rang, waking me from a deep sleep during which I was having a nightmare about dealing with the U.S. Health Department. The woman on the phone said, "I'm calling from O'Hare, and I have your suitcase here but I'm afraid I can't send it to you."

"Why not?" I replied in a stupor.

"Well, I don't have any record that you ever flew with us."

"But you just said that you have my suitcase," I said.

"Well, that doesn't qualify as evidence that you flew with us."

"So what *do* you suppose it means that you have my suitcase?"

"Well, I need documentation."

Then it dawned on me that they had flown the turkey, I mean suitcase, to O'Hare, and that Midway had the documentation. Finally, she believed that the suitcase she had should be sent to me. She then said, "Well, I'll send your suitcase to you, but I don't know if I can get it out today or not."

So I figured she had it coming. "Say," I said, "did you happen to notice if there was any blood coming out of that suitcase?"

She became quiet. She had been pretty verbal up until then. Finally she said nonchalantly, "Why?"

"Oh, no reason," I said offhandedly.

Needless to say, my suitcase arrived at my door within the hour. The turkey was okay except for the legs, which had defrosted slightly. The day after we returned home, my mother-in-law cooked it and served it to some of my father-in-law's relatives she had never really liked.

And I decided I would remember to use the "blood coming out of the suitcase" approach again should they ever lose my suitcase in the future. It's a lot cheaper than a GPS.

45

The Woman with the Easily Assembled, Beautifully Lit Christmas Tree

I just love your Christmas tree," I said while observing a beautifully decorated tree at my neighbor Kristen's house. "I wish I could do more around the holidays, but dealing with trees is so time-consuming."

Kristen said, "Well, this one is artificial, and the lights are already on it."

"You're kidding! That sounds so great, but my husband loves a live tree."

"Well, let him know that the lights are already on; it just comes in two pieces, and then it's done. My husband liked live trees too, but I ordered this and put it together myself. It was the easiest thing in the world! You can order it from the Easy Holiday Solutions website."

The next August, I thought I would get an early start on the holidays, so I ordered a two-piece tree with all white lights from Easy Holiday Solutions. Since our tree always has white lights, I knew Michael would never notice.

As Christmas approached, Caroline and I decided to assemble the tree. I opened the box and pulled out the bottom half of the tree. Then I reached back into the box and pulled out the other half. I put them together. I said to Caroline, "This is so much easier than the trees Daddy gets."

"Mommy, why does our tree look like a Christmas bush?"

I stood back to look. Our tree *did* look like a Christmas bush. We had received two bottom halves of a tree. But it was three weeks before Christmas, so we still had plenty of time.

I called the customer service department and received the following recording: "The elves at Easy Holiday Solutions wish you the very merriest of holidays. We take the *stress* out of Christ*mas*." Holiday music came on. As soon as the customer service representative said hello, there was a loud click and my phone went dead.

I immediately called back and again I heard: "The elves at Easy Holiday Solutions wish you the very merriest of holidays. We take the *stress* out of Christ*mas*." The first time, I hadn't noticed how irritating that high-pitched elf voice was. As soon as the customer service representative said hello, there was a loud click and once again, my phone went dead.

After two more tries, I finally got ahold of an elf named Blizzard. He sounded a bit irritable. "Order number, please," he said gruffly. I gave him my order number and explained the problem.

"Are you sure you have two bottom halves? This has never happened before."

"Look"—*you little twerp,* I thought, as I was feeling a little irritable myself—"I'm sitting here looking at a Christmas bush instead of a Christmas tree. How fast can you get a top half to me?"

"You'll have to talk to a supervisor elf for that. Let me get Snowflake."

Snowflake came on with the same irritating high-pitched voice.

I explained the problem again. "Really, I have two bottom halves."

Snowflake said, "I can't imagine you'd make up something that stupid. We'll send you a top half, but there are a lot of orders in front of you. I can't guarantee anything by Christmas." He hung up.

I was excited when the new box arrived late one afternoon a few days before Christmas. Caroline and I pulled out the new top and placed it on the bottom half. It looked beautiful and the pieces fit together perfectly. This was so easy! Michael was going to be totally fooled! I plugged it in.

Caroline immediately said, "Mommy, why are the lights on the bottom half of the tree *white* and the lights on the top half of the tree *colored*?"

"Damn those stupid elves," I thought to myself.

"Okay, I can do this," I said, as Caroline went out to make a snowman. "I'll take the colored lights off the top and replace them with white lights."

Obviously, those horrid little elves had welded the lights right onto the tree. Even with pliers, they wouldn't budge.

I sat down next to the tree and cried. Suddenly, a burst of inspiration hit. "Why didn't I think of this three weeks ago?" I asked myself.

I put the bottom half of the tree back on top of the other bottom half, and got Michael's chain saw from the garage.

I effectively shaped the Christmas "bush" into a Christmas tree.

Feeling very pleased about the outcome, I plugged in the tree. As I did so, a puff of smoke blew out of the electric socket. I quickly unplugged it, realizing that I must have cut off some of the wiring for the lights. Just then Michael walked in from work.

"Honey, what's for dinner? And why do I smell smoke?"

"Smoke?" I yelled. "*Why do you smell smoke?* It's because I bought a fake tree which turned out to be a Christmas bush, and then I couldn't get through to those stupid little elves, and finally Snowflake said he'd send me a top to the tree, and then when I got it the lights on the top of the tree and the bottom of the tree didn't match, and so I put the bottom half of the tree back on the other bottom half of the tree and used your chain saw to make the Christmas bush into a Christmas tree, and when I did that I cut off the wiring to the lights, so when I plugged it in smoke came out of the socket. *And that's why you smell smoke.*"

"That sounds good." He nodded nervously. "I'll just take Caroline to McDonald's and we'll eat there," he said, backing out of the house.

I wish I could get my hands on that annoying elf, Blizzard. I'd like to see how high I could make his voice go then.

46

The Woman Who Has a Better Way to Do Everything (Like Make Jell-O) and Wants You to Know It

The other day, while a neighbor was over for coffee, Caroline called down from upstairs to say that she and her friend, Hailey, were hungry. I made them peanut butter and jelly sandwiches, and Caroline came down and got them and returned upstairs. I emptied the jelly jar and threw it in the recycling bin.

"I can't believe what I just witnessed," my neighbor said quietly. "You're really throwing away that jelly jar?"

"Why wouldn't I?" I asked, perplexed.

She retrieved it from the garbage. "Because you need to first fill it with hot water and shake it. Then you can use the water to make Jell-O."

"But I don't make Jell-O."

"Well, what do you serve for salad and dessert, if you don't make Jell-O?"

"We don't eat that much Jell-O. Besides, you can buy it now in containers that the grocery store makes."

"Do you think grocery stores would use jelly water to make their Jell-O?"

"I can't imagine they would."

"I rest my case. Jell-O without jelly-flavored water is clearly inferior. I would never eat such a thing."

I thought, "I've got to get out of here," and then realized I was in my own home.

"Well," I said cheerfully, "thanks for stopping by. I've got to go somewhere now."

"Where are you going?"

"Well, um, I'm dropping Caroline off at her friend's house and then I'm going to a movie," I lied.

"What are you going to see?"

"Ah, well, I don't remember the name of it."

"I have one question for you. Are you going to buy a small-to-medium-size drink and popcorn, or a large drink and popcorn?"

I'll admit it. I had to find out where this was going. "Probably a large drink and popcorn. Why?"

"Because then you'll have to leave during the middle of the movie to use the bathroom. You should get the small-to-medium-size drink. Unless, of course, you have a weak bladder; if so you should only get a small container and tell them to fill it with lots of ice."

Warming to her theme, she went on, "I always call the movie complex ahead of time and ask which theater the movie is playing in so that I can park close to the exit of that theater. Would you like me to call them for you? I have the phone numbers of all the theaters within twenty-five miles of here programmed into my cell phone. You're not planning to go to a theater more than twenty-five miles away, are you?"

"Ah, no."

"Well, which movie are you going to see at which theater?" she asked, cell phone poised in her hand.

"You know, I'm not sure," I said, getting up and walking to the door. Luckily, she followed.

"When you're about to go in the theater, notice which side has the garbage can, so you don't have to carry your empty popcorn and drink containers as far."

She was actually telling me where to throw away my containers at the theater. What next? Which bathroom stall to use? I decided I had to walk outside to get her to leave.

She followed me out. "And don't forget to close your purse completely after you get into the theater; otherwise, all kind of valuables might fall out. This happened to my sister once fifteen years ago and since then I try to tell everyone to close her purse while she's in a theater; otherwise she might lose something important."

Increasingly desperate, I was now walking down the street.

She followed. "Do you want to know what my sister lost in the theater?" Without waiting for an answer she continued, "She lost her favorite shade of lipstick, Raspberry Ice, and right after that Clinique stopped carrying that shade. That's why you need to be really careful about closing your purse at a theater."

I was now standing in front of her house.

"There's nothing worse than finding the right shade of lipstick only to find out it's been discontinued. That's why I have stored up 137 lipsticks of my favorite shade, just in case they decide to discontinue it."

By now she had joined me on her front porch. Foolishly I said, "A hundred and thirty-seven?"

"Why, yes," she said. "I calculated how long my mother lived, and how long her mother lived, and took into account the exact number of antioxidants I consume each day, and then multiplied that by two, since I go through one lipstick about every six months, and I came up with 137."

I pushed her into her house, shut the door, and held the doorknob in case she tried to get back out.

While I stood holding the knob, she shouted at the top of her lungs, *"And make sure you don't use the first bathroom stall; everybody uses that one."*

47

The Woman Who Has Mirrors Installed All Over Her House So She Can Enjoy the Results of Her Plastic Surgery

Recently, a neighbor invited me over to see her newly decorated home. As I went in, I commented on how spacious her foyer seemed.

"Well," said Melanie, "I just had these floor-to-ceiling mirrors installed all over my house."

"Did you use mirrors to make the rooms look bigger?"

"Heavens, no. I've spent a fortune in the last five years on plastic surgery and wanted to enjoy the results without standing in front of the bathroom mirror all day. I've had everything nipped and tucked and realized that other people were enjoying the results more than I was. Let's take a little tour."

As we entered the living room, I noticed a mirrored grand piano.

"Oh, do you play?" I asked.

"Well, I do now. I bought this piano from Liberace's estate in Las Vegas. Now that I can see myself while I play, I play every day! It seemed pointless before."

She led me into the family room. On one side of the fire-place she'd hung a flat-screen TV, and on the other side a large mirror.

"This is now my favorite room because my husband can sit in his chair and watch television and I can sit in my chair and watch myself."

"Oh, wow."

"I really think it's important to spend quality time with your spouse."

As we walked into the kitchen she said, "I've totally redone the kitchen. I even had mirrors installed on my kitchen cabinets, upper and lower, so that when I'm preparing food, not that I ever do because I don't cook, I can see myself."

"Isn't that a little scary first thing in the morning?"

"I've always felt strongly that personal grooming should be done the moment you get up in the morning. That way you can enjoy the results all day."

As we climbed the stairs, I noticed that mirrors had replaced each of the risers.

"When I first had these installed, I felt it was terribly distracting to see myself in motion. Now it's the best part of my day."

As I watched myself ascend the stairs, I thought about how demoralizing it was to see my own thighs jiggling.

We peeked into the master bedroom, where—you guessed it—there were mirrors everywhere.

As a person who had spent years *avoiding* looking at myself in mirrors, particularly full-length mirrors, I was starting to panic. I felt like I had to get out of there.

As I was getting ready to leave, I said, "I'm a little surprised. I've just never seen a house decorated with so many mirrors before."

"Well, I realized I was spending so much time at the gym just so that I could look at myself in their full-length mirrors. And after all, I'm already a size 2 and my stomach is flat, so it seemed pointless to spend any more time there. So I decided to put the same floor-length mirrors in my home."

I went home shaking my head. I knew there was a reason I hadn't spent much time at the gym. I may be addicted to a lot of things (Dove chocolate, Weight Watchers toffee ice cream bars, Diet Coke), but watching myself in the mirror isn't one of them.

48

The Woman Who Took First Place at the International Napkin-Folding Contest

At the Super Bowl party we recently attended, I noticed that all the cloth napkins had been folded into the shape of regulation-size footballs. I remarked to the hostess that I had never seen anything like it.

"Oh, that's Juliane's creation," she said, "Let me introduce you."

We walked across the room to a woman sitting on the couch, who was showing pictures to the people around her.

I overheard her say to the woman next to her, "This one took third place in Zurich."

I gave the hostess a quizzical look. "Lauren, this is Juliane. Juliane is the winner of several international napkin-folding contests."

I said, "Really! I've never heard of an international napkin-folding contest."

"Oh, yes, there're very popular. And the competition is fierce. Here's a picture of the napkin I folded at the Russian competition in 2004."

Looking at the picture I remarked, "I'm sorry, I can't make out what it is."

She said modestly, "It's actually not literal. It's an interpretation of the poem 'Renascence' by Edna St. Vincent Millay. See, this part right here is the grave. The Interpretive Poetry Design category is always tough, but I usually do okay. This napkin only placed fourth, but then, the Russian judges always cheat."

"There's an Interpretative Poetry Design category?" I was intrigued.

"Of course," she said, as if I had never been out of my house before. "They also have Regional Design, Landmark Design, Interpretive Dance Design, and Interpretive Music Design. Here's a picture of the small English village I did last year at the Regional Design competition in Manchester, England. As you can see, Tudor-style architecture really lends itself to paper-napkin-folding."

"Yes, it really does," I said, impressed. "I had no idea there was so much going on in the napkin-folding world."

"That's the whole problem," she sighed. "For the average person, paper-napkin-folding has become too boring. We need to break new ground and open new frontiers. During the Interpretive Music Design Competition in Hong Kong last year, many of the younger women wanted to bring in music by Christina Aguilera, and I was all for it. Although there's nothing like doing a napkin-folding interpretation of Edvard Grieg's *In the Hall of the Mountain King,*" she said wistfully. "But I suppose those days are over."

"How did you ever become interested in paper-napkin-folding?"

"From reading the biographies of famous paper-napkin

folders, such as Isadora Duncan. Before she became a famous dancer she ranked pretty high in INF (international napkin folding) circles. Her techniques were revolutionary. And Mamie Eisenhower was another pioneer. She had those foreign diplomats in the palm of her hand after they saw her fold a napkin."

"It sounds as if you've become quite famous in the international napkin-folding arena yourself."

"Yes, but I'm thinking of quitting. The competition has become so cutthroat. I never realized how much stress goes into napkin-folding at the championship level. But there is one more competition I'd like to enter, which is the Interpretative Design category in Milan, Italy, this summer. We'll be interpreting the cubistic design of Picasso, which should be fabulous."

"Do you think you could show me how to fold a napkin so it looks like a fan?"

She pretended not to hear me. "I also like to do biblical interpretive paper-napkin-folding. I once depicted the parting of the Red Sea. It was very moving. And here's a picture of the Eiffel Tower that I did last year for the Landmark Design category. It was held in New Zealand and I took first place. I didn't want the Austrians walking off with the top prize three years in a row, so I thought I'd better compete."

Someone walked over and commented on the football napkins she had folded for the party. She said, "It's worth doing something special for your guests."

And I used to think folding a napkin in half and placing it under a fork was doing something special for my guests.

49

The Husband Who Doesn't Ever Want to Open the Refrigerator Door Because that Would Be Wasting Energy

Many husbands exhibit the following behavior:

1. The minute you leave the family room, your husband runs in and turns out the lights, even though you just left to get a paper towel to wipe off the dust on the TV in an effort to see Rob Lowe more clearly in a made-for-TV movie.
2. Because you like to leave a porch light on at night, in the spirit of compromise your husband changes the porch light from a hundred-watt bulb to a five-watt bulb, which wouldn't illuminate King Kong dressed in Reynolds Wrap if he were trying to break into your house.
3. Whenever you open the refrigerator door, before you even feel a chill, you can sense that your husband is on "the alert" and fidgeting until you shut it again. You learn to use the oven only when he's not around.
4. Because he complains about your wasting water, you

have a twenty-five-gallon drum of artesian water set up in the kitchen. This water costs sixty-eight dollars a month, but the water bill goes down thirty dollars a month. He thinks he's saving money on water, only because he doesn't notice a sixty-eight-dollar drum of artesian water in the kitchen.

5. He asks that people enter or leave the house no more than three times a day to avoid heating or cooling the entire neighborhood. Your children and their friends learn to hurl themselves out the door in an emergency-like fashion. You do receive some macabre satisfaction, however, when his mother visits and has chest pains and he won't let the paramedics in because the kids have already opened the front door three times that day.

6. After complaining about the high electric bill, he insists that you shut down the family room and all pile into the car to watch the DVD and do home-work. The next morning he estimates that he saved eight dollars on electricity that night, even though, later that same day, he had to buy a $154 car battery.

50

The Woman Who Is Always Tan and Has a Flat Stomach

I'm always suspicious when the Woman Who Is Always Tan and Has a Flat Stomach calls me up to get together with her. I suspect her motive is that she just looks that much better when she's standing next to me. Against my better judgment, I recently went with her to a movie and then we grabbed a bite to eat afterward. When we got to the restaurant, I ordered the French dip with extra fries, split pea soup, and Key lime pie for dessert. When the waitress turned to her, the Woman Who Is Always Tan and Has a Flat Stomach said, "Actually, I'm not hungry and I never eat when I'm not hungry. I'll just have herbal tea, thank you." The waitress frowned and left.

I stared at her and said, "You're not ordering?"

"I'm not hungry."

I said, "So?"

She confided, "That's why I don't gain weight."

I said, "I haven't been hungry since 1981 but that certainly hasn't kept me from eating. And in 1981 I was only hungry for about ten minutes until they fixed the micro-wave in my dorm."

She shrugged.

I pressed on. "Do you know that when my doctor prescribes medication that has to be taken on an empty stomach, I have to set my alarm for four a.m.? And do you flat-stomach people *understand* that when I got pregnant, I began to show seven hours later?"

She pretended not to hear me.

Not only is she always thin, she is always tan. In her ancestry she was lucky enough to have a great-great-grandparent who was Italian or Spanish. Obviously, my ancestors were only thinking of themselves and not me when they married only other Norwegians. Would it have hurt anyone to marry someone who was not named Lars or Ole so that we could get some color into our skin tones? Sure, it would have required perilous six-month journeys on scurvy-ridden boats to other countries to find mates with darker skin, but that wouldn't have killed them. Well, probably not. Okay there was a good chance they might not have made it, but is that really the point here?

So last year, right before I had to accompany my daughter to the neighborhood pool, I decided to do something about my Scandinavian-colored skin. I decided to make an appointment at one of those spas where they first exfoliate your skin and then apply a tanning cream so that by May I would look less like a cadaver wearing shorts. Actually, a cadaver has more color than I do.

The woman at the spa applied the tanning cream, and I went home and waited three to four hours for my beautiful bronze tan to appear. What happened, however, was that I turned a light, pallid color. This in no way approached the spa's descriptive "bronze" or "tan." I compared myself to my husband, who had not yet been out in the sun at all this year, and I could see I was still lighter than he was. Of course, he tans from the FASTEN SEAT BELT light when he starts his car.

My pallor prompted me to call the spa lady back to inquire about what had happened to my "beautiful bronze glow." She said, "Lauren, when you start out the color of a white laser, you'll probably need several applications to make it up to the shade of 'bronze.'"

"Considering my skin tones, how many applications do you think would be necessary?"

"Maybe sixteen or seventeen. But we don't have that much bronzer on hand. We could special order it, though I doubt I'll be able to get that much."

It's hard to go through life trying to compete with a cadaver.

About the Authors

LISA PERRY and LAUREN ALLISON originally self-published *The Woman Who Is Always Tan and Has a Flat Stomach (And Other Annoying People)* in 2005, winning two awards in the categories of humor and best title from the Colorado Independent Publishers Association. Lisa Perry has a doctorate from the University of Denver and works as a clinical psychologist in private practice. Lauren has her B.A. from Monmouth College and owns an art business. In 2003, they teamed up to speak to women's organizations and businesses. They have appeared on television and radio programs across the country.